the CARPENTER'S *Miracle*

the CARPENTER'S *Miracle*

JUDD PARKIN

Bonneville Books
Springville, Utah

The views expressed within this work are the sole responsibility of the author and do not necessarily reflect the position of Cedar Fort, Inc., or any other entity.

This is a work of fiction. The characters, names, incidents, places, and dialogue are products of the author's imagination, and are not to be construed as real.

ISBN 13: 978-1-59955-420-4

Published by Bonneville Books, an imprint of Cedar Fort, Inc., 2373 W. 700 S., Springville, UT 84663. Distributed by Cedar Fort, Inc., www.cedarfort.com

LIBRARY OF CONGRESS CATALOGING-IN-PUBLICATION DATA
Parkin, Judd, 1952-
  Miracle / Judd Parkin.
    p. cm.
  Summary: A struggling young carpenter heals a young boy and is hounded by the media.
  ISBN 978-1-59955-420-4
  1. Healers—Fiction. I. Title.

PS3616.A7543M58 2010
813'.6—dc22

2010012359

Cover design by Tanya Quinlan
Cover design © 2010 by Lyle Mortimer
Edited and typeset by Melissa J. Caldwell

Printed in the United States of America

10 9 8 7 6 5 4 3 2 1

Printed on acid-free paper

For Marilyn
First, last, forever

And to Claire, Hilary, and Sam
Our three miracles

1

The fish weren't biting, and it was getting cold. Josh stomped his feet for warmth and looked at the waning light through the tiny window of the shack. "Follow me, and I will make you fishers of men," he said to himself, his breath steaming in the chilly air. This had been the subject of Father Lovett's sermon, a story Josh had always liked.

Josh could hear a group of boys shouting across the lake. *Must be a hockey game*, he thought. The voices rose and fell in the distance, a combination of taunting and cheerleading. Josh looked at his watch and tried to decide if he should call it a day or give it another few minutes. He'd been sitting in the shack for nearly five hours, and all he had to show for it was a couple of nibbles. The brisk, damp air was beginning to cut through his parka, so he would be forced to leave soon whether he wanted to or not. Josh had heard on the radio that this was one of the coldest Decembers in Wisconsin history, and he could believe it. He rubbed his hands together and looked at the small hole in the ice. *Give it five more minutes,* he said to himself. *You never know.*

He reeled in his line to check the bait and saw the worm had been snatched away by a fish that hadn't even tugged on the line. With a sigh, he pulled another night crawler out of the dirt-filled coffee tin and stuck its squirming body on the hook. He dropped the line into the small hole and watched it disappear into the dark water. *Five more minutes.*

Suddenly, the boys' voices grew louder. *Some argument about the game,* Josh thought. But as he listened more closely, he realized they were calling for help. Alarmed, he jumped to his feet and tossed his pole into the corner. He opened the door and looked out.

Two of the boys saw Josh and waved frantically for him to come. Josh realized something was very wrong, and his heart began to race. He closed the door to the shack and broke into a run over the frozen expanse. As he got closer to the boys, he could see the panicked expressions on their faces.

"What's wrong?" Josh shouted, still at a distance.

"Luke fell through the ice! We can't see him!" yelled a brown-haired boy in a red down jacket.

When Josh reached the boys, he saw a dark patch of water near one of the goal nets where the ice had cracked. The boys stared nervously into the water.

Struggling to catch his breath, Josh turned to a boy in a green parka. "How long's he been under?" he demanded.

A boy said, "I don't know—a couple of minutes?" He looked to the other boys, and they shrugged uncertainly.

His mind racing, Josh turned to the boy in the red down jacket and ordered, "Go get help." The boy nodded and ran toward town.

Josh tore off his jacket and threw it on the ice. The cold evening air cut through his shirt like an electric current. Inching toward the edge of the broken ice, Josh shivered as he peered into the water. His heart sank when he could see no sign of the boy. For a moment he was paralyzed by indecision. The boys looked at him, their eyes wide with fear.

"What should we do?" asked the boy in the green jacket, biting his lip.

Without answering, Josh leaped into the hole in the ice. The freezing water hit his body like a hammer, and his muscles tightened instantly. He opened his eyes and looked around, but the light was too dim to see more than a foot in any direction. He waved his arms blindly, hoping to make contact with the submerged boy. Nothing. His heart pounding with fear and cold, Josh swam to the surface and gasped for air.

A boy in a plaid jacket yelled, "Do you see him?"

Josh shook his head, took a deep breath, and disappeared again below the water line. This time, he dove toward the lake floor ten feet away. When his hands touched the muddy bottom, he swatted wildly in all directions but found nothing. Darting to his left, he felt something brush his outstretched hand—the boy's arm. Josh grabbed the limb with one hand, and the boy floated toward him.

He was clearly unconscious, his body a dead weight. Josh hooked his hands under the boy's arms and tried to drag him toward the surface. The body wouldn't budge. Josh's chest was exploding and he knew if he didn't get the boy to the surface soon, they would both be breathing in lake water. He tugged several times, but one of the boy's feet seemed to be caught. Finally, with a violent jerk, Josh pulled him free. Holding the boy tightly, he kicked with all his might toward the distant light.

When they broke through the surface, Josh looked at the boy's face. His eyes were closed and his skin was a ghostly blue. Josh searched for an escape route. The ice at the edge of the hole was brittle. The boys were shouting at him, but his ears were filled with water and he couldn't understand what they were saying.

Pulling the boy behind him, Josh swam to the edge of the ice on the shoreside and tried to climb onto it. The ice broke, and the two of them sank again into the freezing lake. Josh inhaled a mouthful of water and came up coughing, struggling to keep the boy's head above the surface. Another attempt failed, but on the third try, the ice held, and Josh scrambled onto the frozen surface, hauling the boy after him.

He looked down at the boy's face, which showed no signs of life. Shivering from the cold, he lifted the boy into his arms and stumbled toward the bank. The boy was young, no more than twelve. Josh desperately tried to remember the CPR he had learned. He lowered the boy onto the snowy bank and began pressing hard on his chest, hoping to push water from his lungs. There was no response from the boy, who was deathly still. Josh clamped his mouth to the boy's and tried to force air down his throat. This produced no results, so Josh sat up again and pumped four more times on the boy's chest. Again, nothing.

The boy's friends ran around the goal posts and joined Josh on the snowy shore. They watched him, their eyes dark with dread. They all jumped when a distant siren split the evening air. Josh continued pushing steadily on the boy's chest, all the time shouting, "C'mon, breathe!" But for all of his efforts, the boy continued to lie motionless on the cold bank.

2

Sarah was filing papers at her desk in the bank when she got the terrifying call that Luke had been taken to the emergency room. A Sergeant Kurowski—or Kowalski (it was hard to tell since the man's words were a jumble)—called and told her about Luke. Sarah walked numbly toward her friend Alice, two desks away. Alice looked up at her friend and knew immediately something was wrong.

"Luke's in the hospital," Sarah said. "Can you drive me there?"

"Sure," said Alice, jumping to her feet and locking her desk all in one motion. "What happened? Is he okay?"

"I don't know," replied Sarah. "The police officer who called said there'd been an accident."

Alice frowned, not liking the sound of that. She

helped Sarah put on her coat and gently steered her toward the back door of the bank and into the parking lot.

For the first couple miles of the drive, neither woman spoke. Sarah stared ahead at the twilight landscape. The silence became unbearable to Alice, so she turned to her friend and said, "I'm sure it's nothing, honey. You know boys—probably just a couple of stitches."

Sarah nodded without answering. She felt sick and had to keep her hands clasped firmly in her lap to stop them from shaking. When they reached the emergency room entrance, both women were alarmed to see an ambulance and a fire department paramedic truck sitting by the entrance, their lights revolving eerily in the dark. Sarah gave an involuntary gasp, and Alice put a comforting hand on her arm. Alice pulled the car into a parking space, and the two women hurried into the hospital.

In the admitting area, everything was chaos. Paramedics rushed into a back room, followed by a nurse. Three police officers stood in the hall-way, locked in an urgent conversation. One of the policemen pulled out his cell phone and started to dial but stopped when he noticed Sarah and Alice.

Pocketing his phone, he turned and walked toward them.

"Ms. Quinn?" the policeman asked. "I'm Sergeant Kurlanski. We spoke on the phone."

"Yes—where's Luke?" Sarah asked.

Sergeant Kurlanski cleared his throat uneasily and said, "I need to talk to you. There's been an accident."

"Yes, you told me on the phone," Sarah said impatiently. "Where's my son? I want to see him."

Out of the corner of her eye, Sarah saw several of Luke's friends sitting in the waiting room. Before the policeman could answer her, she walked toward the boys. Alice and the policeman had no choice but to follow. The boys stared at Sarah, their faces pale with dread. Sarah turned to a brown-haired boy in a red down jacket.

"Jeremy," she said, "what happened to Luke?"

The boy looked at Alice and the policeman, pleading for their help. No one spoke. The policeman gently placed his hand on Sarah's arm and said, "Please, Ms. Quinn, I need to speak with you alone."

Sarah turned to him, alarm growing in her eyes. The policeman led her to a small office off the admitting area. They stepped into the room, and the door behind them swung shut with an ominous click.

Alice watched them disappear and then turned to the brown-haired boy. "What happened?"

The boy shrugged nervously and said, "We were playing hockey, and Luke fell through the ice."

Alice started to speak again, but she was stopped by a muffled cry from the small office. She and the boys looked in the direction of the sound. Her mind racing, Alice turned back to the boys.

"We don't know what's going on," said a blond boy. "But when we got him out of the water, he wasn't breathing."

Fearing the worst, Alice nodded and rushed to the office. Through the window of the closed door, she saw Sarah sitting with her face buried in her hands. The policeman sat next to her, holding her arm.

Struggling to compose herself, Alice turned to survey the frantic activity in the reception area. A man wrapped in a blanket stood watching her across the hallway.

"Are you a friend of the family?" the man asked.

"Yes," Alice replied. "Who are you?"

The man shook his head sadly. "I—I'm terribly sorry. Everybody did all they could—it was just too late."

The door behind Alice opened, and Sarah emerged with Sergeant Kurlanski at her side. Sarah fell into Alice's arms and whispered, "He's gone." Alice held her friend tightly as Sarah dissolved into tears.

Sergeant Kurlanski cleared his throat and said, "We can have someone take you home, Ms. Quinn. We'll handle all of the arrangements for you."

Sarah broke her embrace with Alice and turned to the policeman. "I want to see my son," she said.

Kurlanski stared at his feet uncomfortably and replied, "That may not be the best idea, Ms. Quinn."

"He's my son," Sarah said firmly. "I want to see him."

Sergeant Kurlanski nodded and began to lead her down the hall with Alice following a few steps behind. The man wrapped in the blanket stepped toward them.

"I'm so sorry," he said.

Sarah turned and looked at the man. He had an angular face and soft, kind eyes. "Who are you?" she asked.

"This is Josh Carey," Sergeant Kurlanski said. "He pulled your son out of the water."

"I wish I could have saved him," Josh said helplessly.

Sarah stared at him for a long moment before saying, "Thank you—thank you for trying."

Josh nodded sadly. Sarah, Alice, and Sergeant Kurlanski turned and continued down the hall. When they reached the door at the end, Sarah stopped for a moment, gathering her strength. She turned toward Josh.

"Will you please join us?" she asked him.

Josh didn't know what to say. He looked at the policeman, who nodded.

"Sure," Josh said, tossing the blanket in a nearby chair.

The four of them entered the back room. Two doctors and a nurse stood over a gurney, talking in hushed tones. When they noticed Sarah, they fell silent. Sarah saw her son's body covered with a sheet, and her knees buckled. The policeman steadied her, and they slowly made their way toward the gurney. The doctors and the nurse stepped aside.

Sarah stood over her son and pulled back the sheet. The boy lay on the gurney, his eyes closed and his skin a dullish gray-blue. Gently, she leaned down and gathered his small body in a firm embrace. She held him tightly, and her shoulders shook with silent sobs.

Josh, Alice, and Sergeant Kurlanski looked at each other, uncertain what to do. After a few seconds, the policeman placed his hand on Sarah's shoulder.

"Please, Ms. Quinn," he said softly, "let us take you home."

At first it seemed Sarah hadn't heard him. But after a moment, she nodded and lowered her son onto the gurney. She brushed back his hair and leaned down one more time to kiss his forehead. Then, taking hold of Sergeant Kurlanski's arm, she started for the door, wiping the tears away from her swollen eyes.

Josh stared down at the boy. He stepped forward, put his hand on the boy's shoulder, and said quietly under his breath, "I wish to God you could have lived, kid."

Just as Sarah and the policeman were about to go out the door, they heard an odd choking noise. Sarah turned quickly and saw an astounding sight: her son still lay on the table with his eyes closed, but his body convulsed with coughing.

Everyone in the room froze. They looked at each other in disbelief and then moved cautiously toward the boy. He writhed on the gurney, coughing and gulping for air. With a cry, he gagged and spit up a mouthful of water. The violent motion threw him into a sitting position, and he blinked open his eyes.

"What happened?" Luke asked groggily. "Where am I?"

For a moment, everybody in the room was too stunned to speak. Luke looked at the wide-eyed group and shook his head, as if to clear it.

"Is this the hospital?" the boy asked. "What am I doing here?"

Without answering, Sarah ran and held Luke tightly, too amazed to cry or speak or do anything but hold him. Luke was embarrassed by his mother's display of affection in front of strangers.

"Mom," he said, "c'mon, let go. I'm okay."

Sergeant Kurlanski gaped open-mouthed at the scene in front of him. "What the heck happened?" he sputtered at last.

The nurse pointed at Josh and said, "He put his hand on the boy's shoulder and the boy came back to life."

Sergeant Kurlanski looked questioningly at

everyone in the room and then turned to Josh. "Is that true?" he asked.

"Yes," Josh said tentatively, "but I didn't do anything."

"You did," the nurse insisted. "You touched the boy and said something to him."

Alice nodded in agreement. "It's true, he did. I saw it."

"What did you say?" demanded Sergeant Kurlanski.

"Just that I wished he could live," Josh said sheepishly.

"You said 'God.' I distinctly heard you say 'God' in there somewhere," the nurse said.

"Maybe I did. I don't know," Josh said.

Sergeant Kurlanski stepped toward Josh, looking at him as if he was an alien. Josh shifted uncomfortably, aware that everyone in the room was staring at him. Sarah loosened her grip on Luke and smiled at Josh through grateful tears. Kurlanski moved closer to Josh and looked closely into his eyes.

"I've been on the force twenty-two years, and I've seen a lot of strange things," said the policeman. "But this is the first time I've ever seen anyone rise from the dead."

Luke looked around the room in confusion. "Dead? Who was dead?" he asked.

No one answered the boy. Josh shifted uneasily and said, "I really didn't do anything,"

"Yes, you did!" shouted the nurse. "You brought this boy back from the dead, and I saw it. We all saw it! It's a miracle!"

Josh felt a sinking sensation as the collected group converged upon him, patting him on the back and congratulating him. He didn't know how to respond. He didn't feel as if he'd done anything, much less performed a miracle. Sarah looked at him, her eyes shining.

"Thank you for my son's life," she said quietly.

Embarrassed by all the attention, but very glad the boy was alive, Josh smiled at Sarah.

3

*J*ack Reardon finished the AP article and then read the headline a second time: "Man Brings Boy Back from Dead."

Reardon took a sip of coffee and stared thoughtfully at the bank of muted televisions on the wall opposite his desk. On the center television was the close-circuit feed of *Inside Look*, the highly rated program that Reardon produced. He stared at the ghoulish images of a derailed roller coaster, but his mind was elsewhere. After a couple of seconds, he leaned forward and hit the intercom.

"Yes, Mr. Reardon?" said a disembodied voice.

"Tell Delia I want to see her," said Reardon.

He leaned back in his chair and skimmed the AP article one more time. Just as he finished, there was a rap at his door. Delia Tynan stood in the doorway, and he waved her in.

"What's up, boss?" Delia asked, throwing herself down on Reardon's plush couch.

"I've got a hot one for you," Reardon replied, giving her the clipping in his hand.

As Delia read the article, her face darkened. When she finished, she looked at Reardon with a puzzled expression and said, "This is a joke, right?"

"Absolutely not," answered Reardon. "This is a big story. I feel it in my gut."

"Jack," Delia began warily, "you're not actually asking me to cover this are you?"

"Yes."

"But I'm overwhelmed with the stories I'm already covering," Delia protested. "Besides, there's a war on, in case you hadn't heard."

"There's always a war going on some place," Reardon replied sanguinely, "but how many times do you see a guy raise a kid from the dead? And right before Christmas?"

Delia stared at him in disbelief and then said firmly, "No. No way. Assign somebody else to this. I'm not wasting my time on some story about a phony miracle."

"It isn't phony," Reardon insisted. "The kid

had no vital signs for over an hour, was legally declared dead, and then this guy does a laying on of the hands—or whatever you call it—and, *bingo!* Suddenly, the kid's coughing up water and breathing."

"I tell you, it's bogus," Delia insisted.

" 'There are more things in heaven and earth, Horatio, than are dreamt of in your philosophy,' " said Reardon, smiling.

"Don't quote Shakespeare to me," Delia snapped. She muttered to herself, "There's gotta be some other explanation. There's no such thing as miracles."

"There were six witnesses, including two doctors and a nurse," Reardon said emphatically. As an afterthought he added, "And a cop."

"Oh, then it must be true," Delia said sarcastically. "Sounds to me like a case of group hypnosis."

She looked again at the AP article in her hand and shook her head.

"It's a gift—I'm telling you," Reardon said.

"Didn't you train me to 'beware of newsmen bearing gifts'?" Delia asked.

"Sure, sure, sure," Reardon said impatiently, "but this is different, my darling little Rottweiler. This is something I'm handing you on a platter.

By the time you're done with this story, you'll be thanking me. This is exactly the kind of piece the Chairman loves."

Delia cocked an eyebrow and looked at him skeptically. "The Chairman? Really?"

"Are you kidding?" Reardon asked. "It's his favorite meal. Schmaltz on Wonder Bread."

"Well—" said Delia uncertainly.

"If the raising the dead angle wasn't enough," Reardon continued, "the guy's initials are J. C."

Delia nodded. "Hokey, but okay—so?"

"Get this—the guy's also a carpenter," Reardon said, sitting back in his chair with a satisfied smile on his face.

"Really," said Delia, her interest mildly piqued.

"And the kid's name is Luke."

"What's that got to do with anything?" Delia asked.

"Nothing, I guess, except I'm pretty sure it's biblical. We'll get our fact checkers on it," Reardon replied. He leaned toward her and spoke in confidential tones as if adding the final flourish, "And if all this weren't enough, this whole thing happened in a town called Bethany."

Delia stared at him blankly. "So?"

"That's the town where Jesus was born!" Reardon exclaimed.

Delia shook her head. "You're thinking of Bethlehem."

Reardon frowned and said, "Are you sure of that?"

"Positive."

Reardon waved his hands impatiently. "Bethany, Bethlehem, whatever. It's close enough. The main point is this is a great Christmas story—tragedy and resurrection, all tied up in a nice red bow. You know this is the kind of thing people eat up at this time of year. They go crazy for all that upbeat human interest nonsense. All I'm asking is for you look into it."

"Like what—make a few calls?" Delia asked.

"No, like pack your bags," Reardon replied. "You're on a flight this afternoon to Wisconsin."

Delia stared at him in amazement. "You're unbelievable," she said at last. "You're shameless!"

"Aren't I?" said Reardon happily.

Delia turned away from him and stared gloomily at the New York City skyline. "You owe me big for this, Jack."

"Of course, I do, honey," Reardon said. "Now you better get going. Your flight leaves at two—oh, and don't forget to take a warm jacket. I hear Wisconsin's pretty chilly this time of year."

Delia stared at Reardon as if she wished he would burst into flames. She shook her head in disgust and left the office without a word. After she was gone, Reardon leaned back in his chair and looked at the AP article again. When he finished reading it, he tossed it on his desk and cheerfully started humming "Jingle Bells" to himself, a small smile on his face.

4

Josh had become a celebrity, and he didn't like it at all. News of "The Miracle" had spread like wildfire through Bethany into the larger world. After the story broke on the AP, he was swamped with calls from news outlets around the country. Two Milwaukee TV stations sent reporters to interview him, and he'd done phone interviews with *USA Today* and more newspapers, magazines, and bloggers than he could count. Everyone, it seemed, wanted to talk to him.

The articles that followed made Josh cringe. A lot of pieces called him "The Miracle Man," and a newspaper in Albuquerque titled their story, "A New Messiah for Christmas?" Josh tried to discourage this kind of thing, but it was no use—people wrote what they wanted to. The more he protested, the more the reporters praised his "humility" and "saintliness."

Josh was religious in a very general way—his mother had called him a "fair-weather Episcopalian"—but he was sure he wasn't a saint.

The circuslike atmosphere in Bethany disrupted every aspect of Josh's life. He was two weeks behind schedule finishing the cabinets in the Barons' kitchen. The Barons repeatedly assured him that the work could wait until the New Year, but Josh felt duty-bound to finish the job before then. He was also behind on several other projects and he felt as though he'd never catch up. Just as frustrating was the fact that he hadn't had time to go fishing since the day of the accident, and a number of his friends had recently landed near-record catches. The fish had suddenly begun biting with an unexpected vigor; it was as if even they had picked up on the excitement in the air.

Sarah and Luke joined Josh in many of the interviews. He had not known them before, although he recognized Sarah from having seen her around town. When she told him she worked at the bank, he realized they must have crossed paths dozens of times. Luke was baffled by the attention he was getting because all he remembered of the entire experience was waking up in the hospital. In his mind, there was nothing miraculous about it. To him, the entire episode of "coming back from the dead" was nothing more than a brief, strange dream that ended with a lot of people making a fuss over him for reasons he didn't fully understand. But he enjoyed all the attention and cheerfully answered the interviewers' questions.

After a week of nonstop interviews, Josh, Sarah, and Luke were tired of hearing themselves talk. As they were leaving one interview session, Sarah turned to Josh.

"Are you as sick of this as I am?" she asked.

"And then some," Josh replied.

Sarah smiled. "With all the craziness that's been going on, I don't feel like I've done anything to really thank you."

Josh shook his head. "Of course you have," he replied. "If anything, you've embarrassed me by talking so much about what a hero I supposedly am. I'm not. I just did what anybody else would have done in the same situation."

"I'm not so sure of that," she said. "Please let me make you dinner—it's the least I can do."

Josh was a bachelor with no cooking skills, so the offer of a homemade meal was tempting. He also wanted to get to know Sarah better—she was a smart, interesting woman, and Luke seemed like a good kid.

"It's a deal," Josh said. "Just give me a date."

"Tomorrow night?" Sarah asked.

Josh tried to mask his surprise. "That would be great," he replied. It seemed to him his voice had a waver in it, and he was worried he sounded like a geeky teenager who'd never been on a date.

Sarah smiled with pleasure. "Seven o'clock good for you?"

"I'll be there," Josh replied. "Can I bring anything?"

"Just you." Sarah smiled.

With a wave, she and Luke climbed into their rusted red Honda Civic. Josh waved back as they pulled out of the parking lot. Feeling foolish, he watched until their taillights disappeared around the corner. When the car was gone, Josh looked skyward and saw a cloud cover obscuring all but a handful of stars. *Definitely more snow*, he thought. He inhaled deeply and made a wish. "Don't let me do anything stupid," he said under his breath.

5

Delia's flight to Milwaukee was delayed two hours at Kennedy Airport because of storms in the Midwest, and this did not make her happy. When she and her two-man crew, cameraman Seb Ballard and soundman Phil Dorney, finally boarded their plane, they were already tired and grumpy. An hour into the flight, the plane hit bad turbulence, which made everyone onboard a little green around the gills. It was not a promising start to the trip.

When the plane finally cleared the storm area, Delia stared out at the lights twinkling on the ground below.

"All the fly-over people," she said to herself.

Seb heard her and said in mock protest, "Hey, I'm from Oklahoma. I'm one of those fly-over people."

"Not anymore," said Delia.

"Once a fly-over person, always a fly-over person," said Seb with a shrug. "Where you end up living doesn't matter."

When the plane finally landed in Milwaukee, they had to sit on the runway an additional forty-five minutes waiting for a gate to open. By the time Delia and her crew piled their luggage into their rental car, it was well after dinnertime. The three of them were tired and hungry, but they decided to make the two-hour drive to Bethany before getting something to eat.

The decision to postpone dinner proved to be a big mistake. The roads were icy, and it took them closer to three hours to reach Bethany. When they hit the city limits, it was nearly nine o'clock, and everything in town was closed except for Mac-Gowran's Tavern and a gas station at the far end of town. Just to be sure, they drove up and down the main drag twice, but there wasn't an open restaurant in sight.

"This is unbelievable!" fumed Delia. "Whoever heard of an entire town being closed up by nine o'clock at night? What do these people do here? Hibernate?"

"They're country folk," said Phil, who'd been

raised on a farm and was familiar with the ways of small towns. "They get up early, so they turn in early."

Delia rolled her eyes at Phil and gestured for him to pull into a parking spot in front of Mac-Gowran's Tavern. The lights were still on, but when they entered the tavern, they were dismayed to find the owner, Ray MacGowran, putting chairs on the tables.

"Sorry, folks," he said, "we're closed for the night. Last call was a half hour ago."

"Last call at eight thirty?" Delia said incredulously. "You close that early?"

"Well, on the weekends we sometimes stay open as late as ten, maybe eleven," said MacGowran, a trifle defensively. "Depends on the customers. Last Fourth of July we stayed open 'til nearly one o'clock."

"Wow," said Delia in mock awe.

"You folks looking for a drink?" MacGowran asked. "I suppose it wouldn't kill me to serve you a round."

"Actually, we were looking for something to eat," Delia said.

MacGowran shook his head. "Sorry, the cook went home at seven—her granddaughter was sick.

Kitchen's closed, but I got pickled eggs and pretzels if that helps you any."

Delia looked in disbelief at Seb and Phil, who shrugged. She turned back to MacGowran and said, "Thanks. Okay, we'll take three bags of pretzels, three eggs, a dry martini on the rocks and—" turning toward Seb and Phil, she gestured for them to place their order.

"Two draught beers," said Seb.

MacGowran nodded cheerfully and went behind the bar to round up their order. He was an older man, on the heavy side, but he walked with a spring in his step at the prospect of a little close-of-business trade.

"A martini," said MacGowran, rubbing his hands together. "Haven't made one of those in a long time—vodka and vermouth, right?"

Delia nodded grimly. "With a twist a lemon, if you have it."

"Sorry, lemons are out of season," replied MacGowran, "but I got some lemon juice."

"Forget the lemon," said Delia, slumping into a chair. She looked around the tavern at the animal head trophies mounted on the walls and shuddered.

As he busied himself making the drinks,

MacGowran chatted cheerfully with his guests. "You folks just passing through?"

"No," answered Delia. "We're going to stay around for a few days."

MacGowran gave them an appraising look. "I expect you're here about the miracle. You must be newsfolk."

"You could say that," replied Delia cautiously. "What do you know about 'the miracle'?"

"Same as everybody else, I guess," said Mac-Gowran, drawing the beer. "I wasn't there. The six people who were there said the Quinn boy was deader than dead for over an hour. Then Josh Carey touched him, said some sort of prayer, and the boy come back to life."

"Do you believe it?" asked Delia.

MacGowran frowned thoughtfully as he placed the drinks on a tray. He carried them to the table and put them before his three clients. After looking at them for a moment, he finally spoke.

"I wasn't there," said MacGowran, picking his words carefully, "so I can't properly say. But I've known those folks all their lives, and I've never known any of them to be a liar."

"Meaning?" prompted Delia.

"Meaning," said MacGowran, "if they say it happened that way, then it happened that way."

"But do you think it was a miracle?" asked Delia.

"Oh, I don't honestly know," replied MacGowran. "Miracles have been pretty sparse around here in my lifetime. But, yeah, I suppose this is as about as close to a miracle as I've ever seen."

"Can I quote you on that?" said Delia.

"As long as you mention the tavern," replied MacGowran with a twinkle in his eye. "And make sure you spell it properly as 'Mac,' not 'Mc.' Otherwise folks will think we're lowland Scots. Bugs me when people get it wrong."

Delia pulled out a pad of paper and began writing quickly. "MacGowran, spelled Mac," she said aloud as she wrote. She clicked her ballpoint pen and leveled her gaze at MacGowran. "Do you know where I can find Josh Carey? I'd really like to speak with him."

MacGowran looked at the threesome and nodded a little warily. "Sure," he replied at last. "He lives on Fig Street in the old Methodist church."

"You've got to be kidding," Delia said. "He lives in a church?"

"That's right," nodded MacGowran. "He's not a religious nut or nothing. His mother's illness nearly broke him financially, so he bought the old church cheap when the Methodists moved across town to their new place. He's doing a nice job of restoring it."

Delia looked at Seb and Phil, her eyes glowing with glee. She then turned back to MacGowran and said, "Keep talking—this is too good."

6

Midway through dinner, Josh dropped a big serving spoon and chipped off a small piece of his plate. While trying to catch the fumbled spoon, his elbow knocked over the gravy boat, spilling au jus sauce all over the starched white tablecloth. Josh was horrified by his clumsiness, and his face flushed a deep crimson. He tried to help Sarah as she mopped up the au jus, and in doing so he nearly tipped over the flower arrangement in the middle of the table. Luke couldn't suppress a laugh, but he fell quickly silent when Sarah shot him a dark look. Josh sank into his seat and shook his head in disbelief.

"I'm really sorry," Josh said. "I don't know why I'm being so clumsy. I'm just sick about chipping your plate."

"Don't worry about it," said Sarah, trying to wave it away.

"Maybe you can perform another miracle and restore it," said Luke with a mischievous smile.

"Luke," said Sarah, giving him a warning glance. She turned back to Josh. "Don't think anything of it. It's just an old plate."

"These are antique plates," said Luke helpfully. "They're real old."

"An antique," moaned Josh. "You must think I'm an idiot."

"Not at all," said Sarah.

"You have to let me replace it," Josh said.

Sarah shook her head doubtfully. "I don't think you'd be able to," she said.

"Then let me repay you some other way," he implored.

"Okay," she replied. "You can buy me dinner this weekend."

Josh almost dropped his fork in surprise. "Dinner?" he asked. "You'd have another meal with me after this?"

"I'll wear something waterproof," Sarah said, smiling.

While Josh and Sarah cleared the table, Luke went into the living room and started flipping through channels on the TV. He came upon a Milwaukee station that was just beginning its evening news broadcast. "Hey," he called into the kitchen, "it's on!"

Josh and Sarah hurried into the living room. The three of them sat huddled together on the couch, and Josh was conscious of being very close to Sarah. Their elbows touched, and he jumped as if he had received an electric shock. After they settled back down, Josh stole a sidelong glance at Sarah. She sensed his gaze and turned to him with a smile. He felt foolish, as if he had been caught doing something inappropriate. His cheeks felt hot, and he realized he was blushing again.

After several breaking news stories, the anchorman introduced a segment that had been taped the day before. A photo of Josh, with a halo superimposed over his head, was projected on the screen behind the anchorman. Josh groaned loudly and buried his face in his hands.

"It's a nice picture," Sarah protested, doing her best not to laugh. "You look good in a halo."

"It's lucky my dad's dead. This would have killed him," said Josh miserably.

Luke, who enjoyed seeing himself on television, shushed them, and they watched the rest of the segment in silence. Images of the lake, the town, and the hospital flashed on the screen, as well as various townspeople talking about "the miracle." The piece hit all the same notes as the earlier stories—death and resurrection, faith and miracles—and called Josh's deed "the greatest Christmas gift of all." The story ended on another photo of Josh, this time with a Santa Claus hat badly superimposed on his head. Though the photo was meant to be flattering, it made him look like a pinhead. Sarah and Luke couldn't stop from bursting into helpless laughter.

"Thanks a lot," said Josh. "Ha-ha-ha."

"You have to admit, it's pretty funny," said Sarah, wiping away tears of laughter.

"Come on, Santa. Cheer up," said Luke, as he and Sarah fell again into side-clutching convulsions.

Josh stared at them and their laughter eventually subsided. "I won't be able to show my face in town," he said glumly. "Maybe I'll just move."

"Don't forget your reindeer," said Sarah, an impish smile on her face. Luke gave a loud bark of laughter, and the two of them sank back on the couch, giggling helplessly. Josh tried as best he could to glare at them, but it was no use. With a resigned shrug, he slumped backward onto the couch and laughed with them.

7

I'm in hell," said Delia into the phone.

"I'm sure you're exaggerating," replied Jack Reardon on the other end of the line. "I'm told Wisconsin is absolutely charming this time of year. Very Grandma Moses."

"If you think you're being funny, you're not," said Delia sullenly. "Look up *backward* in the dictionary, and you'll see a picture of this place. They don't even have a Starbucks."

"Savages," said Reardon in mock sympathy. "Have you found a place to stay?"

"Oh, yes, a charming place," said Delia sarcastically as she gazed around her cramped, dingy motel room. "A rustic little resort called 'Bide-a-Wee' on the highway. I'm in the presidential suite."

"That's good," said Reardon. "Have you located our man?"

"Not yet," said Delia. "But I've talked to a couple of people who know him."

"And?"

"And they think he walks on water," she replied.

"Seriously?"

"Scout's honor," she replied. "It's like I said—group hypnosis. These people buy the miracle thing hook, line, and sinker."

"That's great."

"You don't say!" snapped Delia. "But where's the story? We can't report a miracle really happened here—in the town that time forgot. We'll be laughed out of the business."

Reardon thought about this for a moment. "Well, you'll think of something, my adorable Venus Flytrap. But first off, you have to find our guy as soon as you can. I don't want one of the other networks to beat us to the punch—in fact, I'm surprised nobody has."

"Don't worry, Jack," said Delia. "I know where the guy lives. I've got him in my sights."

"Then fire away," said Reardon happily.

8

When Josh stopped to get coffee at Rose's Café the next morning, he hoped to remain as inconspicuous as possible. But the moment Rose saw him come through the front door, she called out from across the café.

"How come you wore that Santa hat on the news?" she asked.

Josh forced a smile, painfully aware that everyone in the café was staring at him. "I didn't wear it. They superimposed it on a photo of me."

"Well, you shouldn't let them," said Rose, shaking her head. "It made you look like a fenderhead."

"I didn't get a say in the matter," replied Josh. "They just did it." He sat on a stool and signaled to Luther, the lazy-eyed counter waiter, that he wanted some coffee. Luther nodded, brought a pot of coffee over to Josh, and poured him a cup.

"I didn't mind the Santa hat so much," began Luther thoughtfully, "but I couldn't figure out how they got the halo to float above your head in that other picture."

Josh and Rose shared a look; Luther wasn't the sharpest tool in the shed. "Weren't you listening, honey?" asked Rose. "Josh wasn't actually wearing the Santa hat or the halo. The TV people superimposed that stuff on him."

Luther shook his head, confused. "What? They, like, hung it from a wire?"

"No," said Josh patiently. "It was a special effect, like in the movies."

"Ohhhh," said Luther, finally getting it. "Like that Gollum guy."

Josh nodded. "Sort of," he said. He wanted to change the subject, so he opened his newspaper and pretended to read. Luther seemed not to notice and continued talking.

"Well, my dog still isn't doing too good," he said. This seemed to come out of nowhere, but so did most of what Luther said.

"That's too bad," replied Josh, not looking up from his paper.

"Yeah," said Luther. "His back left leg has never been right ever since he got his foot caught in that squirrel trap."

Luther's dog, Toby, was perhaps the only creature in town more dim-witted than Luther. Still, Luther loved the dog, and Josh felt bad for him. "I'm sorry to hear that," he said.

"Sure do wish somebody could do something about it," said Luther wistfully.

"Have you taken him to the vet?" asked Josh

"Yeah," the tall man answered sullenly. "Vet's no help. He says a bone must have got broke and healed wrong. He can't do nothing."

"That's a shame," said Josh, sipping his coffee.

"I don't suppose you'd fix him, would you?" asked Luther.

Josh gave Luther a puzzled look. "What do you mean?"

"You know—fix him," said Luther.

"And how am I supposed to do that?" asked Josh.

"Oh, I don't know," said Luther. "Put your hands on him? You know, like you did with the Quinn kid."

Josh stiffened as he realized where the conversation was heading. "Luther, I'm really sorry about your dog, but you have to understand, I'm not a miracle worker."

"Well, they said on the news—"

"I know what they said on the news." Josh smiled. "But it isn't true. I don't know what happened with Luke Quinn. I'm as confused about it as anyone. I'm really glad he's alive, but I'm telling you, I didn't have anything to do with that—it just happened."

Luther nodded as if he understood. "Sure do wish you could help my dog," he said, proving he hadn't understood a thing.

Josh sighed and closed his eyes. Luther watched him closely, wanting to believe that Josh was saying a prayer for his dog. After a moment, Josh opened his eyes and pulled out his wallet. "So do I," he said, "but I can't." He threw a dollar on the counter, stood up, and moved toward the door.

Luther opened his mouth to say more, but Rose cut him off. "Stop bothering Josh," she said. "You got an order up."

An hour later, as Josh put the finishing touches on the Barons' kitchen cabinets, the conversation with Luther was still bugging him. Did Luther really think Josh could heal the dog? Even more troubling was the idea that perhaps Luther wasn't the only one who had such thoughts. When he walked into the café, he'd noticed something unnerving in the other customers' faces—he saw friendliness, yes, but also a certain amount of—what? Awe? Wariness? Fear even? Josh wasn't sure if any of this was real, or if he was simply imagining it. He put down his tools and stared at his hands. He had a scrape on the knuckle of his right index finger, and there was a faint scratch on his left palm, but otherwise they looked like normal hands. *These are not the hands of a miracle worker.* He looked around the quiet kitchen, uncertain if he'd said the words or merely thought them. There seemed to be another presence in the kitchen, but when Josh spun around to check, he saw that he was alone. He shook his head. *I must be going nuts*, he thought. *Next thing, I'll be hearing voices and speaking in tongues.* He picked up a screwdriver and began tightening the cabinet door over the oven.

Josh saw Tom and Lydia Baron pull into the driveway alongside the kitchen. They were retired teachers, and they looked like a salt and pepper shaker set in their identical parkas and running suits. As Lydia climbed out of the car, she spied Josh through the window and gave him a happy wave. He started to wave back, but Lydia disappeared from view. A split second later, she came bustling into the kitchen with Tom trailing behind her.

"Don't these look nice?" said Lydia, gesturing at the cabinets.

Tom, who was not a big talker, nodded and said, "Great."

The three of them stood in silence for a moment, admiring the cabinets as if they were paintings in a museum. Lydia smiled expectantly at Josh, who felt a need to fill the awkward silence. "I'll be done in just a bit," he said. "Only a couple of more doors to put on."

"Isn't that wonderful?" said Lydia to Tom, who nodded. "The perfect Christmas present." She patted Josh's right hand affectionately, but then quickly recoiled as if she had touched a burning kettle.

"Are you all right?" Josh asked.

"Oh, yes," said Lydia. "The cold is making the arthritis in my hands act up something terrible. Can't get them warm—feel."

She thrust her hands toward Josh, who reluctantly took hold of them. They were freezing. "Yeow," he said. "You're not kidding. They're like ice."

"Yours are nice and warm," said Lydia, rubbing her hands against his. "What'd you do, stick them in the oven?"

Josh laughed. "No, just good circulation, I guess."

Lydia smiled and gave his hands a playful shake before releasing them. An odd look came over her face, and she flexed her hands. "That's strange," she said slowly.

"What?" asked Josh.

"My hands don't hurt anymore," she said.

"That's great," said Josh.

Lydia looked at her hands again and shook her head in amazement. "This is the first time all day they haven't hurt," she said, leveling her gaze at Josh. "What did you do?"

"Nothing," replied Josh.

"You must have," insisted Lydia. She walked toward Josh and stared searchingly in his eyes. "Is this another one of your miracles?"

Josh began to shake his head slowly at first, but as Lydia and Tom continued to stare at him, he shook his head more forcefully until he looked like a bobble-headed doll whose head was about to fly off.

9

Sarah realized she had been staring at the same home loan application for ten minutes without reading a word of it. She had been thinking about Josh and how awkward he'd been the night before. Had she done something to make him feel uncomfortable? She bit her lip and tried to focus on the document in front of her, but it was no use. The figures were like hieroglyphics. She looked around the bank to see if anyone had noticed her daydreaming. A canned version of "Winter Wonderland" played faintly in the background and everyone appeared to be busy with work—everyone except for Alice, who was looking at her with a knowing smile. "Earth to Sarah," said Alice. "Do you read me?"

Sarah shook her head. "Very funny. I'm just preoccupied with this application."

"Sure you are," said Alice. "You're riveted by it. Your intensity is awe-inspiring."

"Oh, shut up," said Sarah with a laugh.

"Let me guess," said Alice. "He's tall, dark, and came to dinner last night."

Sarah nodded ruefully but didn't speak.

"What?" Alice asked. "The evening was a bust?"

"No, no," replied Sarah. "It was fine, just fine. It's just that—" Her voice trailed off.

"What?" demanded Alice.

"I don't know," answered Sarah. "Everything was great except he acted like I had something contagious."

Alice nodded. "Well, you know men. Most of them aren't housebroken."

"No, it was more than that—he was jumpy all evening," said Sarah. She paused for a long moment before looking at her friend and asking, "Alice, am I unattractive?"

Alice rolled her eyes and gave a long-suffering sigh. "Please, I should be so ugly. Unless this guy's a complete idiot—and I don't think he is—you'll go out again."

"We are," said Sarah. "Saturday."

Alice grinned triumphantly. "Well, there you are."

"I asked him," said Sarah.

"But he said yes, right?"

Sarah nodded.

"See," said Alice. "I told you he wasn't an idiot. I've got a good feeling about this guy."

Sarah smiled and turned her attention back to the application on her desk. She stared with determined intensity at the numbers on the paper and started thinking about what she would wear Saturday night.

10

The first time Delia Tynan saw Josh Carey, he was walking through downtown Bethany waving his arms and talking to himself. He seemed oblivious to the outside world as he carried on an intense, one-way conversation. *Is this guy a nutcase?* she wondered. *He doesn't look like a crazy person—in fact, he's rather handsome,* she thought. At the end of the block, Josh made an abrupt turn into MacGowran's Tavern and disappeared from view. Delia checked her watch and saw it was eleven on the nose. *A little early in the morning to start drinking,* she thought. *Maybe he's a lush.*

Delia signaled for Seb to steer the car into a parking space. "Let's stop here."

"Are we having lunch already?" asked Phil, who was always hungry.

"No, I've spotted our guy," said Delia. "He just

went into MacGowran's." Once the car settled into its parking space, Delia opened her door and climbed out.

"You want us to go with you?" inquired Seb.

"No," said Delia. "I don't want to spook him. Wait here."

Seb killed the engine, and Delia slammed her door. As she cut across the street, she fished in her pocket for her small notebook. She looked quickly at her notes—Carey, Josh; thirty-three; carpenter; home Bethany, Wisconsin; also birthplace (?); parents (?); and several phone numbers. As she approached MacGowran's, she closed the notebook and stretched out her hand to push open the double-hinged saloon doors. Without warning, one of the doors swung swiftly outward and hit her in the face. She heard a sickening crunch and saw a burst of white light. For several long seconds, she had the odd sensation of falling a great distance while also remaining in the same place. She felt a jolt and realized she had fallen flat on her back.

Sarah looked up and saw a blurred figure. Her nose was throbbing, and when she touched it, she felt something wet and warm. Her vision swam into focus and was alarmed to see that her hand was covered in blood. She looked up again at the figure and realized it was Josh Carey. He was talking to her, but she couldn't hear him. Had the blow to her nose somehow made her deaf? Josh was backlit by the entrance-way light of the tavern, a half-crescent halo of light at the crown of his head. Slowly, the sound of his voice faded in as if someone had turned up the volume. Delia smiled at him.

"You're better looking than I thought you'd be," she said.

"Excuse me?" asked Josh, dumbfounded. This was the last thing he expected the woman to say.

"Your pictures don't do you justice," said Delia with effort. Her tongue felt thick.

"Do we know each other?" asked Josh.

"We do now," said Delia, extending her hand. "Delia Tynan."

"Josh Carey," he said as he took her hand. He felt slightly absurd shaking this woman's hand as she lay on the sidewalk and looked with concern at her bloody face. "I'm really sorry about this. We need to get you some ice."

"As long as it comes with a martini attached," said Delia.

Josh braced his hand under her right elbow and helped her struggle to her feet. She stood shakily, and they made their way into the tavern.

Ray MacGowran froze in horror when he saw a blood-streaked Delia walk through the door. He carried a low personal injury insurance premium on his place, and a nationally known reporter being injured on the premises held the potential for financial ruin. In record time, MacGowran procured a pack of ice and a stiff martini for Delia, all the while fussing over her comfort and well-being. As MacGowran flew nervously about the tavern, Josh stole a quick glance at Delia.

"Have we met before?"

Delia shook her head. "No, but I get this all the time. People think they know me because I'm on television."

Josh snapped his fingers in recognition. "That's where I know you from—you did that show about the quintuplets."

"Sextuplets," corrected Delia. "But who's counting?"

"So you're famous," said Josh.

"So are you," countered Delia.

"Yeah, famous," said Josh. "I think I've used up my fifteen minutes."

"Hardly," said Delia. "That's why I'm here—I want to interview you."

"Of course," said Josh, his heart sinking. "I didn't figure you'd come here on vacation."

"Hardly," said Delia sarcastically. Josh frowned, so she quickly added, "But it's a lovely town, and I can imagine coming here on a holiday. It's very Grandma Moses."

"It's what?" asked Josh.

"Never mind," said Delia, pressing on. "Your story has caught the imagination of the country, and people are dying to know more about you."

"Well," said Josh, "I don't know about that."

Delia put down her ice pack. "Trust me," she said, "they are."

Josh shook his head. "Look, Ms.—" he couldn't conjure her name.

"Tynan,"

"Ms. Tynan, I respect your opinion," Josh said, "but I think enough is enough. I'm pretty much done with this whole media thing."

"No!" blurted Delia, almost shouting. Not wanting to seem desperate, she recovered quickly and said, "I mean, why would you say that?"

"Everything's been blown way out of proportion," said Josh. "All this phony miracle stuff."

Delia focused on him like a laser beam. "Are

you saying it wasn't a miracle?"

"Yes—I mean, no," fumbled Josh, waving his arms in frustration. "I have no idea what it was. All I know is I'm sick of talking about it and I think people are sick of hearing about it."

Delia shook her head fiercely. "You are so wrong about that, Josh—may I call you Josh?"

"Everyone does."

"Let me explain why people can't get enough of this story."

"Please do," said Josh. "I can't figure it out."

Delia turned toward the bar and waved her empty glass for Ray MacGowran to see. "A refill, padre," she said, and then turned back to Josh with a winning smile. "Where would you like me to start?"

11

Josh's mother sat in her chair, watching the snow fall in the field outside her window. Her slate-gray hair and pale complexion was reflected in the window, but she didn't notice her own image. Instead, she watched one snowflake after another float to the ground and disappear into the sea of white. She had been doing this all day. Every half hour, a dark-haired nurse checked in on her. The young woman would linger in the doorway for a few seconds, and once she was satisfied everything was fine, she continued on her rounds.

The shadows outside grew longer, and the snowflakes seemed to glow in the darkening afternoon. Josh's mother marveled at the wonderful variety of it all. When it was nearly dark, she spotted something startling against the dark silver sky: three snowflakes locked together in a triangular formation. The three joined flakes weaved in front of the window on their way to the ground. She had never seen anything quite so amazing. When the three flakes finally disappeared into the blanket of snow, she felt a twinge of sadness. She stared for a long time at the spot where the flakes had landed.

There was a knock at the door, but she didn't look away from the snow. The person in the doorway rapped again, and she didn't want to seem rude so she turned around. A young man she didn't recognize stood just outside the room. "Hello," he said. "How are you today?"

"I'm very well," she answered. "I've just seen the most remarkable thing."

The young man pulled a chair alongside her and sat down. She told him about the three snowflakes and pointed to the spot where they'd fallen.

He looked out the window and pretended to see the trio of snowflakes. "That's wonderful," he said.

"Isn't it though?" She smiled, but then a cloud crossed her face. "I'm sorry—I don't recall your name."

"It's Josh, Mom," said the young man.

"What a nice name," she said. "I've never met anyone with that name before."

Before he could reply, she turned back to the

window. He cleared his throat, hoping to get her attention, but she kept staring out the window.

"Mom—I've had an offer," he said finally, "to go on national television. What do you think?"

The woman smiled at him, her eyes shining brightly. "I just love television," she said with conviction.

"Should I do it?" he asked.

"I don't see why not," she replied. "Nothing bad ever happens on television."

She turned away from him again and stared intently at the falling snow. Josh looked sadly at his mother's finely honed profile and felt very alone.

12

If Alice heard "The Little Drummer Boy" one more time, she was going to scream. The song droned on the grocery store PA, and the dreary "pum-pum-pum-pums" of the male chorus felt like tiny hammer blows on her head. She already had a splitting headache, and this wasn't helping. She looked around the store to see if anyone else was as irritated by the song as she was, but the other shoppers seemed oblivious to the piped-in music. Everyone around her moved in a barely controlled hysteria, grabbing items off shelves, rushing down the aisles, carts banging into carts. Was it her imagination, or did people go a little nuts at Christmastime? She came to a stop in the middle of the frozen food section, closed her eyes, and took several deep breaths. To her relief, "The Little Drummer Boy" came to an end; to her annoyance, it was followed by "Frosty the Snowman," one of the few Christmas songs she hated even more. With a sigh, she grabbed a couple of packages of Weight Watchers lasagna and made her way to the checkout line.

As Alice unloaded her cart, a male voice behind her said, "Hello!" She turned and saw Sergeant Kurlanski, the policeman from the hospital.

"Hi," said Alice, surprised to see him. "I haven't seen you since . . ." Her voice trailed off in hesitation.

"Since the miracle," said Sergeant Kurlanski, completing the sentence for her.

They laughed uneasily. Alice glanced in his cart and saw it was filled with several cases of beer, bottles of rum, and cartons of eggnog. Sergeant Kurlanski noticed her look and said, with some embarrassment, "This isn't for me. It's for our department holiday party."

"Oh," said Alice, nodding.

"I don't drink," volunteered Sergeant Kurlanski. "At all."

Not knowing what to say, Alice smiled. "That's nice."

They fell into an awkward silence as Alice

finished unloading her cart. After a few seconds, Sergeant Kurlanski broke the silence. "So, have you seen your friend and her son lately?"

"All the time," replied Alice. "She and I work together."

"I didn't know that," said Sergeant Kurlanski, making a mental note of this fact. "First Prairie Bank, right?"

Alice smiled and nodded. Wanting to keep the conversation going, Sergeant Kurlanski continued, "Well, I guess you've heard about Josh Carey. Pretty amazing, huh?"

Alice gave him a puzzled look. "What are you talking about?"

"You don't know?" asked the policeman. Alice shook her head, so he continued, "From what I hear, the miracles keep coming."

"What miracles?"

"Well, I wasn't there," began Sergeant Kurlanski, "but I understand he cured some woman's arthritis."

"You're kidding."

"Nope," said Sergeant Kurlanski, shaking his head. "He took her by the hands, did something, and presto—no more arthritis."

Alice frowned, trying to make sense of it all.

"Wow, that seems awfully unusual," she said skeptically.

The policeman shrugged. "It's unusual to see a kid come back from the dead, but we saw that, didn't we?"

Before Alice could reply, the tall, pimply faced checker spoke up. "He also healed Luther Froebler's dog." Alice and Sergeant Kurlanski looked at the young man, who smiled at them sheepishly. "Sorry," he said, "I didn't mean to eavesdrop. Just that everybody's talking about it."

Alice and Sergeant Kurlanski shared a puzzled look. Then Alice turned back to the young man. "How did he 'heal' the dog?" she asked.

"Just by thinking about it," said the young man. "Praying, I guess. The dog had a limp, and now it's gone."

"Are you sure about that?" asked Sergeant Kurlanski.

"Positive," said the checker. "Luther's a friend of mine. The dog is healed, praise the Lord."

"This is all too weird," said Alice.

"You said it," agreed the policeman. He then looked directly at Alice and said, "Can I get your phone number?"

The sudden change in subject caught Alice off

guard. After a brief hesitation, she reached into her purse and pulled out a scrap of paper. She wrote down her number and handed it to him.

"Praise the Lord," said Sergeant Kurlanski with a smile.

13

Okay, where's the dog?" asked Delia impatiently. Her voice was nasal, and she dabbed at her nose with a Kleenex. *If I have a broken nose,* she thought, *I'm going to sue Reardon, the Chairman, and everyone else at the network. What a job, to be in Wisconsin in the middle of the winter—surely there has to be an easier way of making a living.* She followed Luther through the barnyard of his father's farm with Seb and Phil close behind. Seb lugged his camera on his shoulder, and Phil carried his sound equipment in a shoulder bag, both of them walking gingerly on the slick, ice-encrusted snow. Delia's nose still throbbed, and she had a splitting headache.

"He's gotta be around here somewhere," said Luther vaguely. He made some clucking sounds, the kind of noises you would normally use to call chickens. Seb and Phil, who knew a bit about farm animals, exchanged a puzzled look.

"So how did Carey cure your dog—what's his name?" asked Delia.

"Toby," answered Luther. "It was real mysterious. Josh just closed his eyes and said a prayer."

"How do you know he was praying?"

"I can tell."

"And then?" inquired Delia.

"And then, when I got home, my dog was fine," said Luther. "Cured. Josh done it.'

"Huh," said Delia, knitting her brow.

Luther started clucking again. After a few seconds, a mangy mixed-breed dog poked its head out from behind the barn. He stared warily at the humans in the yard while Luther called to him.

"Here, boy," chirped Luther. "C'mere, Toby-boy."

The dog regarded him with suspicion and didn't move.

Luther turned to Delia and said confidentially, "He's a little shy around strangers."

"Aren't we all?" asked Delia irritably. She waved in the direction of the dog. "Can't you make him run or something? I want to see how this puppy's been cured."

Luther nodded conspiratorially, pulled a small package of turkey jerky out of his coat pocket, and opened it. The dog's ears shot up at the crinkling sound of the wrapper. Luther pulled the jerky out of the container and waved it in the air. The dog's eyes followed the movement of the jerky. Delia turned to Seb and Phil and silently indicated they should start filming. The assembled group watched the dog, who did not move.

"Oh, for goodness sake," said Delia finally. "What's the matter with the dog?"

Luther ignored her and continued to wave the treat in the air. "Who wants a snack?" asked Luther brightly, taking a bite of the jerky. The dog, watching Luther's every move, slowly edged out from behind the barn. After smacking his lips in an exaggerated way, Luther tossed the jerky into the middle of the pen. Unable to contain himself any further, the dog scampered toward the jerky. Delia watched the dog intently, and her heart sank when she saw he had a pronounced limp—in fact, he was barely able to walk. When the dog reached the jerky, his back left leg gave out altogether, and he collapsed onto the frozen muck, chewing happily on his snack.

Luther turned to the assembled group, beaming. "See," he said proudly, "all cured."

"You've got to be joking," said Delia in disbelief. "That dog needs a walker." She signaled for

Seb and Phil to stop recording.

Luther recoiled as if he'd been slapped. "What do you mean?" he asked, sullen and hurt.

"I mean, he's not cured!" said Delia, getting angry. "In other words, no miracle!"

"Oh, I don't know about that," said Luther defensively. "You should have seen him before. He was a lot worse. He couldn't hardly walk."

"He still can't," replied Delia.

"I tell you, it's a miracle," said Luther stubbornly.

Delia shook her head and then ran her hand through her hair in frustration. "Okay, whatever," she said in disgust. "It's a miracle. The most amazing thing I've ever seen. Now I know there's a God."

"Well, of course there is," said Luther.

Delia smiled tightly and leaned toward Luther. "Call me when the dog starts speaking in tongues." She turned on her heel and walked quickly away. Seb and Phil gave Luther a sympathetic shrug and then hurried after her.

"But dogs don't . . ." said Luther in confusion, his voice trailing off. He watched the three people walk up the hill to their car and called after them. "So what's the story?" he shouted. "Am I going to be on TV?"

14

"The red dress makes you look fat," said Luke.

Sarah sighed. "Thank you for your honesty," she said.

"Well, you asked for my opinion," said Luke. "If you don't want to know what I think, don't ask."

Sarah looked at herself nervously in the mirror. "Do I really look fat?"

"No, of course not," said Luke. "It's just that dress—it's all poofy stuff at the sides. It makes your hips look bigger than they are." Then he added, "You're not fat."

"Thank you," said Sarah gratefully. She stared at the red dress in the mirror and had to admit Luke was right—the trim below the waist was unfortunate and it did make her look hippy. She rushed into her bathroom, shed the red dress, and put the green one back on. As she came out of the bathroom, the doorbell rang.

"Oh no! That's him," she said, her voice tensing in panic. "He's early again—what is it with this guy?"

"Maybe he's desperate," said Luke.

Sarah rolled her eyes. "Thanks, you're a real morale booster. Go let him in, please. I'll be right down."

Luke left the bedroom and bounded down the stairs. As he threw the front door open he said, "You're early again. Mom's not ready yet." Once the door was fully open, he was surprised to discover a pretty, dark-haired woman standing on the front porch instead of Josh. Luke smiled at her. "Sorry, I thought you were someone else."

"You must be Luke," said the woman. She extended her right hand in introduction. "Delia Tynan. What an amazing thing you've been through—how did it feel to come back from the dead?"

Luke shook her hand and shrugged. "It was okay, I guess."

"Such a handsome young man," said Delia. "Is your mother home?"

Luke blushed at being called handsome. He

turned and ran up the stairs, calling as he went, "Mom! Someone wants to talk to you." He circled around the banister and disappeared into an upstairs room.

After a few seconds, Sarah came hurrying down the stairs toward the front door. As she approached Delia, she said, "Can I help you?"

"My name's Delia Tynan, and I'd love to speak with you, if you can spare a moment," replied Delia. "I'm a reporter with—"

"*Inside Look*. I know. I recognize you from that quintuplets show," said Sarah.

"Sextuplets," said Delia. "So you're familiar with our show. That's great. Can you talk for a few minutes?"

Sarah bit her lip. "I really can't," she said. "I'm going out and I need to get ready."

"Sure, I understand," said Delia. "Is there any time soon we could speak? I'm sort of on a deadline."

"Well—" began Sarah, but she was interrupted by the sound of footsteps coming up the walk. Josh emerged into the light, clearly surprised to find Delia on Sarah's front porch.

"What are you doing here?" Josh asked Delia.

Sarah gave Josh a puzzled look. "You know each other?"

"Yes," replied Delia.

"Not really," said Josh simultaneously.

"We've met," explained Delia.

"Are you stalking us?" Sarah demanded of Delia.

"No—she wants to do an interview with me," explained Josh. "And with you too."

Sarah's wariness of Delia turned instantly to dislike. "No thanks," she said finally. "No more interviews."

"It's not really an interview," pleaded Delia. "I would just like to talk with you."

"Isn't that the same as an interview?" Sarah asked.

"Not really," answered Delia. "More of a conversation, a dialogue. It can be whatever you want it to be. I'm flexible."

Sarah shook her head. "No thank you." She turned to Josh and said, "We need to get going. Our reservation's at seven."

Delia watched them with a tight smile on her face. When Josh took a step toward the house, Delia halted him by putting a hand on his shoulder. "Tell her what an opportunity this is," she said.

"Okay," replied Josh noncommittally.

Sarah took note of Delia's hand on Josh's shoulder and frowned.

"It's a win-win situation for everyone," insisted Delia.

"All right," said Josh. "I'll keep that in mind."

Delia stood on the front porch and smiled at them, seeming reluctant to leave. She looked back and forth between Josh and Sarah and then said, "I seem to be interrupting something here. Are you two going out on a date?"

Sarah gave Delia a steely look and said, "I really don't think that's any of your business. Good night."

Delia hesitated for a moment and then said, "Night." She started down the walkway but then turned and spoke to Josh. "Tell her about the package—it's a very generous proposal."

Josh nodded patiently. "I will."

Delia gave them her most winning smile, swung open the front gate, and disappeared down the street.

After she had gone, Sarah turned to Josh. "Why didn't you warn me she was coming?"

"I'm sorry. I didn't know myself," replied Josh defensively.

"I don't like having reporters show up unannounced on my doorstep."

"I understand."

"Is she a friend of yours?" asked Sarah.

"No," said Josh, "I barely know the woman. I've talked to her once. Why are you giving me the third degree?"

Sarah sighed deeply and smiled. "I'm sorry. I'm a bit on edge, I guess," she said. "I just wish everything would go back to normal, like before."

"You and me both," said Josh. "I'm not ready to be the new Messiah."

Sarah laughed. "That must be a lot of pressure."

"It's murder," said Josh. "I just can't get the walking on water thing down."

"Practice makes perfect," Sarah said brightly.

"Should we go?" asked Josh. "It's nearly seven."

"Our reservation's not until seven-thirty," answered Sarah. "I just said seven to get rid of her."

Josh raised his eyebrows, impressed. "Clever."

"Let me get my things," said Sarah. "You care for a drink? There are sodas and juice in the fridge, or, if you prefer, you can turn some water into wine."

"Plain water's fine," Josh said with a smile.

15

$\mathcal{D}$elia wandered through downtown Bethany, lost in thought. The town's Christmas lights sparkled brightly in the cold night air, and she could hear an instrumental version of "Silver Bells" somewhere in the distance. She was in a bad mood and only vaguely aware of her surroundings. She couldn't figure out Josh Carey. Most people were dying to be on television and were easy to manipulate—she'd never met anyone who wasn't begging for his fifteen minutes of fame. Was Carey playing hard to get? His reluctance seemed real, but then again, it might be a negotiating ploy—she couldn't be sure.

She stopped and took in the sights of the town. Quaint didn't do it justice. It looked like a parody of Bedford Falls. The only thing missing was the Bailey Building and Loan. Delia suddenly felt a wave of overpowering homesickness for New York. She wanted to be in a dark, sleek bar drinking martinis, and lots of them. Martinis with a twist of real lemon, none of this lemon juice stuff MacGowran's served. Suddenly, her cell phone went off in her coat pocket, startling her. She checked the number and frowned: it was Reardon. For a moment, she considered not answering the call, but she knew she had no choice. With a wince, she clicked her phone on.

"Jack," she said brightly, "what a nice surprise."

Reardon's voice on the other end was coolly business-like. "Delia, give me good news."

"What do you want to hear?" she asked, stalling. "Everything here's coming up roses."

"Have you locked down an interview with the miracle man?" Reardon demanded.

"Absolutely," said Delia with assurance. She bit her lip at this lie, listening to see if there were any telltale signs of disbelief from the other end. When Reardon did not reply, she plunged ahead. "Everything's set. We're just working out some details."

"That's good," said Reardon, "because a little birdie told me Gil Graham is in Bethany."

At the mention of Graham's name, Delia's heart

began to pound like a kettledrum. Graham was the anchor of *Deadline*, and it was very bad news if he was in Bethany. Affecting a tone of unconcern, Delia said, "Oh, is Gil in town? I haven't seen him."

"That's the word on the street," said Reardon. "Something about an exclusive with a guy whose dog was cured by our miracle maker—what's that about?"

Delia snorted. "It's a wild goose chase, Jack. I've seen the dog, and it's a gimp—there's no story there."

"I'm very glad to hear it," said Reardon. "From here in Gomorrah, it sounds as if miracles are heavy on the ground in Bethany. One half expects to hear that fishes are being turned into loaves of bread. There was an unconfirmed report on Fox that our fellow cured some woman of crippling arthritis."

Delia's mind was racing; she knew nothing about this. She decided to brazen it out. "A pack of lies, Jack. I've looked into this angle and there's nothing to it." She cringed, waiting to see if he believed her.

There was a long pause on the other end of the phone before Reardon spoke. "I'm so glad to hear it. But don't let any grass grow under your feet,

Lois Lane. With these wildcat rumors popping up, every national news service is sending in a team. Lock this guy down."

"It's done, Jack. Trust me," said Delia.

"I don't want to hear that Gil Graham has gotten an exclusive with this guy," said Reardon in a level voice. "It would be very bad for everyone if Graham scooped us. The Chairman wouldn't like that at all."

The threat of this statement hung ominously in the air. Ignoring the queasy feeling in her stomach, Delia said, "Not gonna happen. I've got this thing nailed."

"I'm so glad to hear it, my bright little star," said Reardon cheerily. "Make Daddy happy."

The line went dead. Delia gritted her teeth and cursed under her breath. She hated it when Reardon spoke to her with this sort of cheery condescension. Taking a couple of deep breaths to slow her racing heart, she looked around and tried to decide what she should do. One thing was certain: she had to find Josh Carey and make a deal.

16

All the way through dinner, Josh felt as if his tie was pulled too tight, which was strange because he wasn't wearing a tie. In the first half hour of the dinner, he found himself telling Sarah his entire life story in what seemed to him to be extremely dull detail—his garden-variety childhood, his father's death from a heart attack when he was a teenager, his college years, the problems of starting his own business, and his mother's descent into dementia. Sarah listened in silence, and Josh felt sure she was bored out of her mind. When he finished his story, he realized he was sweating; he glanced down and saw that perspiration had begun to stain his shirt. Horrified to find himself in a flop sweat, he rose quickly and excused himself.

As he walked through the bar on the way to the bathroom, he thought he saw a picture of Lydia

Baron on the barroom television. Before he could examine the picture more closely, the image vanished. Why would Lydia Baron be on television? A nice, retired schoolteacher from Bethany, Wisconsin? He wondered if his nerves were causing him to imagine things.

In the bathroom, he doused his face with cold water and then looked at his image in the mirror. With the water dripping from his face, he looked like a melting wax effigy. *Don't screw this up*, he said to himself. *This is a nice woman. Don't bore her. Quit talking about yourself, you moron.* He pulled a handful of paper towels out of the dispenser and dried his face. *Please, God*, he thought, *let this woman like me. Is that asking too much?*

When Josh came out of the bathroom, a man at the bar stood abruptly and moved toward him. Josh had the sensation of having seen him somewhere before. The man was tall and had almost comically chiseled features. He extended his hand as he stepped in Josh's path. "Mr. Carey—Gil Graham. I was wondering if I might have a moment of your time?"

Josh shook his hand. "It depends," said Josh distractedly. He looked over Graham's shoulder at the dining area and saw an unsettling sight: Delia

Tynan was sitting in his chair, talking animatedly to Sarah. Even at this distance, Josh could see Sarah was not happy.

Graham continued to talk rapidly. Josh's focus was split, so he didn't really hear what was being said, but it was something about him being an inspiration to all Americans. Josh winced and tried to step around him. Graham stopped Josh with a gentle but firm hand on his shoulder and thrust a business card at him. He pressed it into Josh's hand and said, "Don't make any decisions before you talk to me. Whatever Delia Tynan's offering you, we'll double it." He smiled at Josh and clapped his shoulder fraternally.

Josh recoiled from the invasion of his personal space. "Okay," he said. He put the card in his pocket and walked back to the dining area. He crossed through the crowded room and came to a stop at his table.

When Delia saw him, she smiled brightly and said, "Oh, there you are. Pull up a chair. I need to talk to the two of you."

"We're in the middle of dinner," said Josh in disbelief. "What are you doing here?"

Delia didn't offer to give him back his seat, but instead waved for a waiter to bring Josh another chair. "I was just telling Sarah what you've apparently neglected to tell her—about the fee I've offered for the two of you to appear on my show. It's a very generous offer, if I do say so—and that's to say nothing of the potential book deal."

"What book deal?" Sarah asked.

A waiter brought a chair from a neighboring table, but Josh waved him away. He turned to Sarah and said, "She's guaranteeing me—us—a large cash payment and a publishing deal if we'll grant her an exclusive national interview."

"No," said Sarah firmly. "Don't do it."

Delia's eyes went wide, but she quickly masked her panic. "Don't make any snap decisions here. You don't want to do something you regret. Let's get you a chair." She started to signal the waiter again, but Josh stopped her.

"I don't need a chair—I want to sit in my own chair and finish my dinner," said Josh. "Please get up."

Delia stood slowly and looked back and forth between the two of them. "Have you made a deal with someone else?" she asked suspiciously.

"I don't know what you're talking about," said Josh.

"Because if you have," said Delia, overriding

him, "we'll double whatever they're offering."

"We haven't made a deal with anyone," said Josh.

"Not that I'm bragging, but *Inside Look* dominates the market in the eighteen-to-forty-nine demographic," said Delia in a rush. "We more than double our nearest competitor in the key women's eighteen-to-thirty-four demo, and we are consistently first or second with men of all age groups."

"What are you talking about?" asked Sarah in confusion.

"I just wanted to give you some sense of our market dominance," said Delia. "Fourteen of our stories have been optioned for features, and three have been made into award-winning films. Well, two won awards—the other was sort of a turkey."

As she continued to tick off her show's selling points, the cell phone in Josh's coat pocket went off. Both women looked at him as he fumbled to get the phone out of his pocket.

"Hello?" Josh listened to the phone for a few seconds, and his face went slack with shock. "I'll be right there," he said, and clicked off.

"What's the matter?" asked Sarah.

"It's my mother," said Josh. "She's had a stroke."

17

By the time Josh reached the hospital, a feathery snow had begun to fall. As he pulled into a space, his truck fishtailed on the slick parking lot surface. He ran into the hospital and went to the main desk. A soft-spoken receptionist directed him to his mother's room on the fourth floor. As Josh dashed toward the elevators, a middle-aged woman in the outer waiting room blocked his path. Josh saw that her face was red and tear-streaked.

"You're Josh Carey, aren't you?" the woman asked. "You saved the little boy."

"Yes," said Josh, not wanting to be rude but in a hurry to get upstairs. He gave her a faint smile and tried to edge his way around her.

The woman clutched his arm desperately. "Please," she began. "My brother was brought in earlier with a massive heart attack. Could you please visit him?"

"What do you expect me to do?" Josh asked.

"What you did for the boy," said the woman, her voice rising with urgency. "Heal him."

Josh shook his head in disbelief. "I'm sorry about your brother," he said haltingly. "But there's nothing I—I have to see my mother." He felt panic course through his body as he hurried to the elevators.

"Please," the woman called after him.

Josh felt hopelessly torn. "I'm sure your brother will be fine," he said, disappearing into the elevator. Once the doors had closed, he slumped against the wall and closed his eyes.

When Josh stepped out of the elevator, he saw Dr. Cheung coming out of his mother's room. A genial Chinese-American of forty, he seemed younger than his actual age. The doctor saw Josh coming out of the elevator and walked toward him.

"Your mother's stable now," Cheung assured him. "But there's considerable swelling in the left frontal lobe region. If it's still so pronounced in the morning, we'll have to operate to relieve the pressure."

Josh winced. "Is she in pain?" he asked.

"No," said the doctor. "Not much consolation, I know, but it's something."

The doctor led Josh into his mother's room. She was lying in bed, her face pale and still. Her mouth and nose were covered by an oxygen mask, and the only sound in the room was the low hum of the monitors by her bed. Josh had a sudden memory of Luke Quinn lying on a gurney in the emergency room of the same hospital. He sat in the chair beside his mother's bed and took her right hand in his. Her skin felt clammy.

Josh turned toward the doctor. "Can she hear us?" he asked.

"Probably not," said Cheung. "She's in a deep coma. We're registering little brain activity."

Josh nodded and turned back to his mother. He wanted to pray, but he didn't know what to pray for. Her condition seemed hopeless; even so, he could not bring himself to pray for her death. He felt a pang of guilt because, in most ways, death would be a blessing. But he couldn't wish for her death. At a loss, Josh said a prayer for mercy.

His mother's body shuddered. Josh looked at Cheung, who shook his head to indicate the movement was involuntary. Josh sank into his chair as

Cheung checked the charts hanging at the end of the bed. Josh turned back to his mother and saw that her lips appeared to be moving beneath the mask. He leaned close to her but could hear no sound. He squeezed her hand tightly and thought, *Mercy.*

The quiet in the room was suddenly broken by his mother's voice. "Joshua," she said hoarsely, her voice muffled by the oxygen mask.

Cheung looked up from the chart in surprise. "What was that?" he asked. "Did she just say something?"

"Yes," said Josh, his eyes fixed intently upon her face.

"That's impossible," said Cheung. "The speech centers of her brain are completely compromised."

The two men edged closer to the bed. Beneath the oxygen mask, Josh's mother once again mouthed words.

Josh and Cheung exchanged a look and leaned closer. There was no sound in the room except the rhythmic whisper of the oxygen machine. A nurse walked into the room and approached Cheung. He quickly signaled her to be quiet. The nurse looked at the two men for some sort of explanation, but they ignored her.

Just then, Josh's mother gave a low moan and said, "Joshua." The nurse gasped, and the two men exchanged a startled look.

Cheung shook his head in disbelief. "This is scientifically impossible. It has to be some sort of involuntary response. I've never seen anything like it—it's amazing."

"You know what's even more amazing?" asked Josh in a thin voice.

Cheung shook his head.

"She hasn't said my name in over two years." Josh turned to look at his mother, who was breathing peacefully into her mask.

18

*W*hen Sarah got home, Luke was sitting in the living room playing a video game. She hung up her coat and heard the sound of gunfire. When she walked into the living room, Luke ignored her. His eyes were locked on the TV screen, where a cop car was chasing two men in a convertible, with both sides blasting away at each other. Sarah leaned down, kissed Luke on the forehead, and then started out of the room. Luke paused the game and asked, "How was your date?"

Sarah thought for a moment. "I didn't go on a date," she replied finally. "I had dinner with a reporter."

Luke frowned. "What do you mean? I thought you were going out with Josh."

Sarah nodded. "So did I." Without any further explanation, she turned and tramped up the stairs.

When she reached her room, she closed the door
and sat on the bed. She stared at her reflection in
the full-length mirror on the closet door. Her face
was drawn, and she thought she looked very, very
old. Talk about bad luck: her first real date in over
two years, and the guy's mother has a health crisis.
Well, maybe it wasn't meant to be, she reflected. She
wasn't sure what, if anything, she should do to support Josh. In truth, she barely knew him. She didn't
know if he'd appreciate her support, or if he would
regard it as some sort of an intrusion. She closed
her eyes and said a silent prayer for Josh's mother.
Help her, she thought, *and help Josh.*

The phone next to the bed rang loudly and
startled her. She wondered who would be calling at
such a late hour, and the thought crossed her mind
it might be Josh. She picked up the line. "Hello,"
she said tentatively.

"Ms. Quinn—Gil Graham here," said the voice
on the phone. "I'm with the news show *Deadline*—
perhaps you've heard of us."

"Yes," replied Sarah, barely masking her disappointment.

"Excellent," Graham said brightly. "I'm calling you because I understand you're close with Mr.
Josh Carey. Is that a fair statement?"

Sarah tensed. "I don't know that we're 'close,' " said Sarah. "We're friendly."

"Friends then," said Graham pleasantly. "Well, I'm calling you because there's been an unconfirmed report tonight that your friend, Mr. Carey, used his healing powers to bring his mother out of a coma. Would you care to comment?"

The words had come in such a rush that Sarah had trouble absorbing them. "What?" she stammered in disbelief. "Who told you this?"

"A reliable source," said Graham. "Would you care to comment for the record?"

"I don't know what you're talking about," said Sarah in frustration. "And, no, I don't want to comment for the record or off the record. In fact, I don't want to talk to you at all." She slammed the phone into its cradle. Then, for good measure, she lifted up the phone and slammed it into the cradle a second time. *What is going on?* she asked herself. *Had Josh somehow saved his mother? Did he really have healing powers?*

She was desperate to talk to someone about all this. She thought for a moment about calling Alice, but then she remembered this was the night Alice had her date with the policeman. She stared at her own reflection again. I *need chocolate ice cream,* she thought to herself, *and lots of it.* She kicked off her shoes, slid her feet into a pair of slippers, and headed downstairs to the kitchen.

19

Josh spent the night in the lounge down the hall from his mother's room. He slept fitfully on a cramped couch, waking up every couple of hours to check on her. Just before dawn, he finally fell into a deep sleep. In his dream, he caught one fish after another. The last fish he pulled in was a huge bass. When he yanked it out of the hole in the ice, it flopped at the end of the line and struck him on the chest. Startled, Josh fell backward, swatting at the air.

A voice said, "Hey, hey—easy there."

Josh opened his eyes and saw an orderly standing over him. Still half asleep, Josh looked around on the floor for the bass that had hit him in the chest. The orderly watched him with curiosity. "You lose something?" he asked.

"The bass," said Josh. "Where'd it go?"

"You're dreaming, Mr. Carey," said the young man. "C'mon, the doc wants to see you."

Josh followed him out of the lounge. Just before he stepped into the hallway, he turned and gave the room a last, quick look—no fish.

The orderly led Josh to a small office near the admitting area and gestured for him to go in. Dr. Cheung sat behind a desk in the cramped room, finishing a call. He hung up the phone and motioned for Josh to sit in the chair on the other side of the desk. The orderly disappeared into the hallway, closing the door behind him.

Cheung sighed deeply. "The news isn't good, Josh," he said, shaking his head. "The swelling hasn't gone down. I'm afraid we're going to have to operate."

Josh slumped in his chair. "There's no improvement? I thought maybe with her speaking and all—"

Cheung stopped him. "I don't know how to explain that, Josh. It doesn't conform to any patterns I've ever seen before—it's an aberration I can't explain. But the fact remains, the pressure on your mother's brain is severe, and the only way to relieve it is through surgery."

Josh absorbed this news as Cheung continued,

"It's an expensive procedure, as I'm sure you can imagine—"

"I don't care," interrupted Josh. "I don't know how, but I'll figure out a way to pay for it."

"—but more important," continued Cheung, "I can't offer you any guarantee of success. Given your mother's condition, even if the surgery is a success, she may never come out of this coma."

Josh shuddered—this was what he'd feared most. He felt alone and frightened, and he wished there were someone he could turn to. He thought of Sarah.

After a few seconds, Cheung spoke. "Josh," he said gently, "do we have your permission to operate?"

Josh nodded and signed the release forms the doctor put in front of him. This done, he went into the hallway and walked in the direction of the cafeteria. When he reached the entrance, he stood for a moment, lost in thought. An idea began to form in his mind. He reached into his jacket pocket and pulled out a business card and his cell phone. Exhaling a resigned sigh, he began to dial.

20

$\mathcal{D}$elia sat in her car scanning the hospital parking lot. Seb and Phil stood fifty feet away near the hospital entrance, their equipment at their side. They were chatting with Gil Graham's film crew and a reporter from ABC. Delia frowned; she didn't like the idea of her team talking to the enemy. Neither Seb nor Phil were rocket scientists, and she was afraid they might say something to give Graham or the ABC guy an edge. *But what could they give away?* she reminded herself. Neither she nor her crew knew anything. All they had from their time in Bethany was some footage of a crippled dog.

Five camera crews hung around the hospital entrance, which was four too many as far as Delia was concerned. News teams from all over the country had descended on Bethany when a rumor spread that Josh Carey had brought his mother out of a coma. It was exactly the kind of feeding frenzy Delia had dreaded.

She looked down the row of cars and could see Gil Graham across the aisle in a red Taurus, talking on his cell phone. She wondered who he was talking to. If he was negotiating with Josh Carey, she would shoot herself—better, she would shoot Graham. A few seconds later, Graham glanced in her direction, and she quickly looked away. Not wanting to appear idle, she pulled her cell phone out of her purse, put it to her ear, and pretended to talk with someone. She peeked in Graham's direction and was pleased to see he was still looking at her. She gave him a bright wave, and he waved back tentatively. *That jerk*, thought Delia. *I bet he's not talking to anyone, either. Well, two can play at this game.* She started laughing uproariously as if the nonexistent person on the other end of her imaginary phone call had just said something wonderfully witty. She laughed so hard, some saliva went down her windpipe, and she alternately choked and laughed. She glanced again in Graham's direction and saw that he was still looking at her. She realized to her horror she probably looked as if she was having some kind of fit. She tried to recover her composure, but she was coughing so hard tears came to her eyes. Just as she was managing to get her hacking under control, the cell phone rang loudly in her ear. She was so startled she jumped, which set off a new round of coughing. As she tried to catch her breath, Delia looked at the number on her phone; it wasn't one she recognized. Warily, she clicked on.

"Hello," she said hoarsely.

"Ms. Tynan?" asked the voice on the other end.

"Speaking," said Delia.

"It's Josh Carey. I want to talk to you about your offer."

Delia shot bolt upright. "When can you meet?" she said. "I'm completely available."

21

$\mathcal{S}$arah felt lightheaded. She sat alone in a back booth of MacGowran's, nursing a glass of white wine and trying to remember the lyrics of "God Rest Ye Merry Gentlemen." She hummed along with the music, occasionally singing a few bars under her breath. The bank's holiday party had been going on for nearly two hours, and the assembled group was getting very merry—too merry. The bank manager was dancing drunkenly with his secretary, and one of the security guards had passed out on the pool table. Compared to the revelers around her, Sarah felt distinctly unjolly.

She looked at her watch and, for the dozenth time that day, thought about calling Josh. Across the room, she saw Alice and her policeman waltzing slowly back and forth in the corner of the tavern. She felt a pang of jealousy. After only one date they were already behaving like love-smitten teenagers, whereas she didn't know if she should call the man who'd saved her son's life.

As she watched Alice and the policeman dance, Sarah saw a figure flash past the front window of the tavern—it looked like Josh. She shook her head, certain her mind was playing tricks on her. But after a moment, the front door of MacGowran's opened, and Josh walked in. She froze with her glass of wine poised in mid-air. Josh stood for a moment in the entryway and scanned the crowd. She watched as he made his way to bar. "God Rest Ye Merry Gentlemen" ended, and Dean Martin started crooning, "Baby, It's Cold Outside." Josh leaned on the bar and shouted something in Ray MacGowran's ear. MacGowran nodded and looked out over the crowd. When his eye fell on Sarah, his face lit up and he gave her a friendly wave. He shouted something to Josh and pointed in Sarah's direction. Josh turned toward her, and for a moment their eyes locked.

Sarah suddenly found herself feeling light-headed. As if in delayed motion, Josh turned away from Ray MacGowran and started walking in her direction. He seemed to float toward her. Sarah had the sensation of being pinned to the spot, and she felt a warm rush of blood to her head. She glanced down at her feet, and they seemed to be very far away from her. When she looked up again, she was surprised to see that Josh was blurry, as if he had suddenly slipped out of focus. She blinked her eyes several times and then slid off the booth and onto the floor with a dull thud.

After what seemed like several years, Sarah opened her eyes again and found herself looking up at Josh and a circle of people. Dean Martin was still singing on the tavern sound system, but it now sounded like he was underwater. *I've always loved Dean Martin*, she thought to herself. Josh reached under her arm and helped her slowly to her feet. She still felt dizzy as she sank back down into the booth. She looked groggily at Josh and could see he was talking, but it was a jumble. She wrinkled her brow and focused on what Josh was saying. Slowly the words began coming in broken bursts: Was she okay? . . . Bad timing, but need to talk . . . Mother very sick . . . surgery necessary . . . could she help? . . . Luke and her to be interviewed . . . Luke to be examined by doctors . . . A hefty fee for all of them . . . Delia Tynan would call her with the arrangements.

When Sarah heard Delia's name, her mind quickly came into focus. "Don't do business with that woman—she's bad news."

Her urgency caught Josh off guard. "Sarah, I don't have much choice," he said. "My mother needs surgery, and I'm broke."

"I can arrange a loan through the bank," said Sarah. "If I have to, I'll give you the money."

Josh was grateful for her offer but shook his head sadly. "I don't think you understand how much money we're talking about here. If I sell my rights to—" He fumbled for the name.

"*Inside Look*," prompted Sarah with disdain.

"—right, then between that and what Ms. Tynan tells me I can get for a book deal, I should be able to stitch together enough money to cover my mother's medical bills."

"What book deal?" asked Sarah. "Is she guaranteeing you a contract? Has she put an actual offer on the table?"

"Well, no," said Josh uncertainly, "but she said it's a sure thing after my—our—interview plays on national television."

Sarah thought about this for a second and then said, "I'm begging you, don't do this."

Alice and Sergeant Kurlanski made their way

through the crowd to the table. "Honey, what's wrong?" Alice asked. "Did you faint?"

"I'm fine," said Sarah. "I'm just tired and the wine went to my head."

"Let me check your vitals," said Kurlanski helpfully. "I'm certified in CPR."

"I'm fine," said Sarah, holding up her hands to keep them back. "This is not a medical emergency. I was just light-headed for a moment, but it's passed." She turned back to Josh. "Please, will you listen to me? No good can come out of this interview. You have to believe me."

"How can you be so sure?" asked Josh.

"Woman's intuition," volunteered Alice.

"It stinks, Josh," said Sarah. "Delia Tynan is trouble."

"I don't have a lot of options here," said Josh defensively. "I don't like the woman either, but I'm in a bad spot, and I don't have the luxury of standing on some sort of moral high ground."

The words hit Sarah like a slap in the face, and she immediately regretted the things she'd just said. "I'm sorry. I know you're in a horrible position," she said. "Tell me how I can help."

Josh looked at her evenly. "By doing one more interview, you and Luke—she wants the three of us. Will you do it?"

"Of course," Sarah replied.

Josh exhaled deeply and nodded. "Thanks," he said finally. "I'll tell them you're in. They want to do this tomorrow."

"Whenever," said Sarah. "I'll make myself completely available."

Josh looked at his watch. "I need to get back to the hospital." He started for the front door but stopped after a couple of steps. He hesitated for a moment and then turned back to Sarah. "I didn't mean to be so abrupt," he said. "It's been a very rough day. Thanks for your help."

Before Sarah could say "You're welcome," Josh turned once again and disappeared in the crowd. After he was gone, Sarah had the sinking sensation that an unseen balance had shifted—but what this balance was, she didn't know.

22

Jack Reardon could barely contain his glee. "He took our low-end money?" he asked with delight.

"Rock bottom," replied Delia on the other end of the line.

"But how did you get him to go for it?" inquired Reardon. "Especially with all the other people chasing this story?"

"I told him it was the best we could do," she said simply. "He seemed to accept that. He didn't even haggle."

Reardon frowned. "You're sure you've got him? How do you know he's not just using our offer to negotiate with Gil Graham or someone like that?"

"I've got a signed contract," answered Delia. "Exclusive national broadcast rights, signed and notarized."

Reardon shot up straight in his chair, laughing

happily. "Oh, my little burrowing insect, you are brilliant!" he cried. "Why don't I pay you more?"

"Yes, why don't you?" asked Delia.

"Network belt-tightening," said Reardon. "We all have to leave a little money on the table, make a few sacrifices."

"Like your home in Tuscany?" asked Delia.

"You know that's a tax write-off," replied Reardon dismissively. "But why quibble about side issues? The point is you are a genius—no, don't object—you are."

"Was I objecting?"

"How soon can you do the interview?" Reardon asked.

"Tomorrow," said Delia. "We're shooting it at his home."

"Good, good," said Reardon, nodding.

"Get this, Jack," said Delia, setting him up for the punch line. "He lives in a remodeled church."

Reardon shook his head in disbelief. "This just gets better and better. It plays right to the heart of the whole new Messiah for Christmas angle. It's uncanny."

"Yes, we could go that way," said Delia. She paused and lit a cigarette. "But there's another way we might go—if you're interested."

Something in her tone made Reardon come to attention. "Talk to me—I'm all ears."

23

The house was quiet when Sarah returned home from the bank party. She climbed the stairs and peeked into Luke's room. He had fallen asleep on his bed, fully dressed with his iPod perched on his chest. She could hear the faint sound of music chiming out of the iPod's earphones. As she looked at her son, she had a heart-stopping memory of his shrouded body lying on the gurney in the hospital. Her throat closed in an involuntary gasp, and her body shuddered. Using all her will, she blocked the image from her mind and forced herself to take a few deep, calming breaths.

Sarah sat on the edge of his bed and gently stroked her son's cheek. Luke stirred slightly and his eyes cracked open.

"Hey," he said sleepily. "What's up?"

"You need to get ready for bed," said Sarah.

"We have a busy day ahead tomorrow."

Luke rubbed his eyes and yawned. "Why?"

"We're doing another interview," said Sarah.

Luke groaned. "Not another one. I'm sick of being 'Miracle Boy.' "

"It'll be the last one, I promise," said Sarah. "It's going to be on national television."

This got Luke's attention. "Really?" he said. "That's kind of cool. So, I'll be famous, huh?"

"I suppose," said Sarah. "Now get your pajamas on."

Luke sat up and groggily pulled off his hockey jersey. Sarah walked into her room, sat on her bed, and took off her earrings. As she listened to Luke rumble around in his bedroom, she thought about the interview with Delia Tynan. She barely knew the woman, but she didn't like her. She wanted to believe Josh felt the same way, but she wasn't sure if he did. Maybe his judgment was clouded by the crisis with his mother. *Is it possible he'd been seduced by this woman?* Sarah wondered. She had to admit that Delia Tynan was beautiful, and she was certainly famous—men could be idiots about these things. Luke appeared in her doorway and gave her a half wave. " 'Miracle Boy' reporting for sleep detail," he said. "Night."

"Good night, honey," said Sarah. "Sleep well."

After Luke had gone, Sarah lay back on her bed and stared at the ceiling. Her mind was racing with the events of the evening, and she had the uneasy sense of having done something wrong. She closed her eyes and took several deep breaths. In a few seconds, she was fast asleep, fully clothed, with all the lights on.

24

The inflated Santa on the school lawn blew back and forth in the morning wind. From his mother's hospital room, Josh sipped a cup of coffee as he watched the Santa roll around. His mother was lying quietly in bed, a network of tubes and IVs running from her frail body.

It had been a long night. After arranging his interview with Delia Tynan, Josh spent the rest of the day at the hospital with his mother. The surgery had taken nearly four hours, and Dr. Cheung assured him things had gone as well as could be expected. Still, the doctor warned Josh, it was impossible to predict the course of her recovery. Everything depended on how his mother responded to the surgery, and the next forty-eight hours were crucial.

He stared at the dressing on his mother's head;

it was encased in gauze, and two small tufts of hair jutted out the back. Her breathing was steady and untroubled. He'd spent the previous night sleeping in a chair, and he ached all over. Looking at his mother, he felt raw with emotion and fatigue. *Please, God*, he thought to himself, *let my mother live. I am not good at praying, and I know you shouldn't ask for things, but let her live.*

Josh became aware of a sudden quickening of the beeps from the heart monitor. He looked up and saw that his mother's heart rate had almost doubled. Surprised, he turned back to the bed. His mother's lips were moving, and it looked like she was whispering. He leaned closer to listen, but the only sound in the room was the insistent beeping of the monitor.

25

The morning had not begun well for Sarah. When the doorbell rang at six-thirty, she woke to discover she'd slept in her clothes. She had a bad case of bed hair, and her head felt fuzzy—not a hangover exactly, but as if her brain had been wrapped in yarn. She struggled out of bed and walked gingerly down the stairs.

She was surprised to discover Delia Tynan and a strange man standing on the front porch. Behind them stood several other people holding cameras and sound equipment. Delia introduced Dr. Voinovich, the man who was going to examine Luke. Sarah was startled to see the doctor. When Delia had told her Luke would have to be examined, Sarah had assumed it would be in a clinic or hospital. She never imagined she'd have to subject Luke to this indignity in their home, early in the morning, before he'd even had a chance to eat breakfast.

"He's still sleeping," said Sarah. "Isn't there another time we can do this?"

"I'm afraid not," replied Delia. "I'm scheduled to interview Josh this afternoon, so, as you can see, I'm dealing with a limited time frame." She smiled with her mouth only, her eyes fixed upon Sarah.

Sarah's first impulse was to tell this woman to go away. But then she thought of Josh's plea for help the night before. Should she call him to confirm that all this was what he had agreed to? Then She remembered he was with his mother in the hospital. *Better to do the interview and be done with the whole thing*, she decided. It wasn't as if she and Luke hadn't been through this before—although never at such an early hour.

Sarah walked upstairs and woke Luke. After a great deal of begging, she managed to coax him downstairs. When they reached the living room, they found it overrun with people. Without asking Sarah's permission, Delia's crew was busily rearranging the furniture and setting up lights. A large burly man carrying three bouquets of Christmas flowers came in through the front door. Two other men arranged unfamiliar needlepoint pillows on the couch; one of the pillows bore the legend "God is Love." Sarah walked across the room to Delia and pulled her aside.

"Excuse me," said Sarah. "What are these people doing to my home?"

Delia smiled pleasantly. "We're just dressing the house to make it look, well, more homey. Doesn't it look nice?"

"What do you mean, 'more homey'?" asked Sarah, offended. Delia saw Luke standing in the living room archway and quickly changed the subject. "There he is," she said, smiling. She grabbed Dr. Voinovich's arm and propelled him toward the boy. "Doctor, this is Luke, the handsome young man who made the miraculous recovery."

Luke blushed deeply as Dr. Voinovich studied him. "We'll have to do a full physical, of course," the doctor said evenly. "Standard procedure."

Sarah put a protective arm around her son. She wanted to tell these people to leave her house. Everything that had happened since the miracle suddenly seemed like a bad dream. She looked at Luke, who was clearly uncomfortable, and she felt a sense of helplessness. *How did this benefit anyone?* she wondered.

Delia clapped her hands together and smiled at Sarah. "I think we should let Dr. Voinovich take a look at Luke. Then we'll do your interview. What do you think?"

Sarah leveled her gaze at Delia. "I think someone should teach you manners," she said.

Delia looked as if she had been punched in the stomach. "I'm sorry," she said. "Have we done something to upset you?"

"Would you care if you had?" asked Sarah.

Delia glanced nervously at Dr. Voinovich. "Yes," she replied with as much sincerity as she could. "Yes, of course I would care. Would you prefer to do your interview first?"

"It doesn't matter," said Sarah wearily. "Whatever you say. But first, my son and I need some breakfast."

Delia nodded. "Of course."

"And I want you and your crew out of my house in an hour," Sarah said.

Delia glanced quickly at her watch. "Sure." She nodded. "We can do that."

Sarah steered Luke toward the kitchen, and Delia called after them. "Would you mind if we shot some B-roll of you eating breakfast?" she asked.

Sarah gave Delia an icy look.

"Bad idea," said Delia, waving it off. "Never mind. Go. Have breakfast, and we'll get set up in here."

As Sarah and Luke disappeared into the kitchen, Delia turned to Dr. Voinovich and silently mouthed the word "testy." The doctor stared at her, his face an expressionless mask.

26

Luther Froebler sat eating his cornflakes while staring at his dog, Toby. Luther frowned because the act of thinking deeply was difficult for him. His face relaxed into a sullen glare as he spoke to the dog. "Who says you ain't cured?" he asked petulantly. "I seen you before, and I seen you now, and what Josh done to you is a miracle."

The dog looked up at him and barked, as if in agreement.

Luther nodded. "Darn right. You know, don't you, boy?"

Toby had no idea what Luther had said, but an idea formed in his head he'd done something good and that he might get some food for this. He sat up and barked again.

Luther smiled. "That's what I say. Forget them newspeople. You can't expect people with no faith to recognize a miracle."

Toby panted and waited eagerly for food.

" 'Pray for one another that ye may be healed,' " said Luther, finishing his cornflakes. "That's what Josh done for you, right, boy?"

The dog stared at him, not understanding a word.

"You know it," said Luther, taking the dog's silence for agreement. "And if those newspeople don't believe it they can kiss my—" He hesitated for a moment before adding, "Acts of the Apostles."

Toby was mad he hadn't gotten the food he thought was coming, so he barked in protest.

Luther took Toby's barking as a sign of unity. "That's right. We won't let them push us around. C'mon, let's go feed the pigs."

Luther stood up, swung the back door open, and headed for the barnyard. Toby watched him go in silence. When he was satisfied Luther was out of earshot, he propped his front legs on a chair and started lapping up the dregs of Luther's cornflakes.

27

Josh blinked into the bright lights and shifted in his chair. Behind the floodlights, several technicians ran around, setting up sound equipment and a small monitor. Josh was uneasy about having this many strangers in his home. He waved at the chaotic scene. "Is all this necessary?"

Delia Tynan looked up from her notes and smiled at him. "Afraid so. Pretty minor apparatus compared to some of the shoots I've done." She smiled again and then turned her attention back to the papers in her lap.

Josh nodded as if he understood, but none of this made any sense to him. "What exactly do you want to talk about?" he asked.

"Oh, standard stuff," said Delia reassuringly. "Ground you've covered before, I'm sure. The

accident, what happened after, people's reactions—
that kind of thing."

Josh nodded again. He felt nervous but wasn't
sure why.

Delia looked at Seb. "Let's do this."

Seb stood up from behind the camera and spoke
to Delia. "Go when you're ready. I'm good."

Phil adjusted the microphone in front of Josh
and Delia and then turned on the audio equipment.
"Me, too," he said. "We've got speed."

Delia turned toward Josh with a bright smile
on her face. He was amazed at how she suddenly
appeared larger than life; the lights seemed to
magnify her entire personality. "So, Josh," she
began, "how long have you known you had healing
powers?"

Josh thought he'd heard her wrong. "Excuse
me?" he said finally.

Delia smiled patiently. "How long have you had
the power to heal?" She said it as if she were talking to a slow child.

"I—I don't know," Josh said, trying to get his
bearings. "I mean, I've never claimed to have the
power to heal."

"Never?" asked Delia skeptically.

"Never," said Josh. "You all said that."

"Who is 'you all'?"

"You—the people in the media," said Josh, exasperation creeping into his voice.

"Isn't that a bit paranoid, Josh?" asked Delia. "Are you claiming there's some sort of media conspiracy?"

"I—no. Of course not," said Josh, deeply rattled by the question. "Not a conspiracy, exactly, just a misunderstanding."

"About what?" Delia inquired.

"You know, about the 'miracle,'" replied Josh.

"So you do believe it was a miracle," said Delia.

"I didn't say that. You did."

"Me?"

"You know," said Josh, losing patience. "The media."

"Ah, the infamous media conspiracy again," said Delia, nodding her head. "This seems to be a recurring theme with you. Do you feel persecuted?"

"No—yes—I mean, no," said Josh. He could feel beads of perspiration on his forehead. "I'm not saying there's a conspiracy. I'm just saying that something happened, and the press called it a miracle. I never did."

Delia nodded thoughtfully for a couple of seconds. When she spoke again, she took a different tack. "So you never claimed to be a 'new Messiah'?"

"Are you serious?"

"Yes."

"Of course I didn't," said Josh, getting mad. He realized he was breathing heavily.

Delia saw he was angry, but she didn't back down. "Why do you live in a church?" she asked.

Josh tensed. "This is not a church," he said, his voice rising. "This is my home."

Delia frowned, as if confused, and gestured at the surrounding area. "It certainly looks like a church."

"It was a church," Josh said. "It's not anymore. It was decommissioned, or de-sanctified, or whatever they call it. Now it's just my home."

"But it was a church, right?" persisted Delia.

Josh sighed. "Yes."

"Do you have some sort of Christ complex?"

Josh couldn't believe his ears. "What?"

"Do you," said Delia, measuring her words carefully, "have some sort of Christ complex?"

Josh rose angrily from his chair and stepped

toward Delia. When he spoke, his voice was icy. "Get out of here."

Delia looked nervously at Seb to make sure the camera was still on. Satisfied it was, she turned again to Josh. "We haven't finished the interview."

"Yes, we have," said Josh.

"You didn't answer my question, Mr. Carey," said Delia.

"What do you want me to say?" Josh exploded. "Should I say, 'Sure, I'm the Risen Lord. I walk on water to amuse my friends, I calm storms when the mood seizes me, and I turn water into wine because it's cheaper than shopping at Walmart'? Is that what you want?"

"Do you believe all that?" Delia asked.

Josh shook his head in disgust and moved toward the camera. When Seb saw him coming, he instinctively took a couple of steps backward. Josh covered the camera's lens with his hand. "Turn this off," he ordered Seb.

Delia's eyes sparkled with barely concealed delight. Seb reached toward the camera to shut it off, but Delia stopped him with a quick shake of her head. "We're not finished, Mr. Carey," she said.

Josh wheeled around to face Delia again. "What

do you want from me?" he demanded.

"The truth," said Delia.

Josh shook his head in disgust. "Don't insult me. I'm just a sound bite to you."

"No, you're not," said Delia with urgency that surprised even her. "A lot of people—"

"Get out!" shouted Josh.

For a moment, everyone in the room was still. At last, Delia looked toward Seb and nodded for him to cut the camera. She turned back to Josh and said, "Please, let's just all calm down and—"

"Get out," Josh said in a whisper. He walked quickly to the front door and opened it. Delia tried to make eye contact with him, but he avoided her gaze. After a moment, she motioned to her crew to pack up their gear. She gathered her notes with an outward attitude of sad resignation, but as she left, a small smile of satisfaction crossed her face.

28

The nurse finished cleaning the room and glanced at her watch. She picked up the remote on the nightstand and switched on the television. As she flipped through the channels, she spoke over her shoulder to the old woman in the bed. "Your son's on TV tonight," she said. "I thought you'd want to see him." She found the channel she was looking for and put the remote back on the nightstand.

Josh's mother lay silently in the bed, her breath shallow. The nurse emptied the stale water from a flower vase. As she refilled it, she looked at the television and saw various shots of Bethany, ending on an eerie image of the lake where Luke Quinn had fallen through the ice. It looked like something out of a horror film. Images of townspeople talking about the "miracle" flashed across the screen. The final person in the sequence was a man named

Luther talking about how Josh had healed his dog.
This was followed by a quick shot of the dog limp-
ing across a barnyard.

"He sure doesn't look cured to me," said the
nurse to Josh's mother. The only reply was the
beeping of the heart monitor. The nurse straightened the sheets and picked up the clipboard at the
foot of the bed. She glanced again at the television set and saw a female reporter interviewing a
pretty young woman and her son—undoubtedly
the Quinn boy and his mother.

"I don't know if you could call it a miracle," said
the woman. She was clearly nervous. The reporter
asked several more questions regarding the nature
of her beliefs: Was she religious? Did she believe
her son had come back from the dead? The woman
shifted uncomfortably with each question, and her
answers were vague.

The reporter appeared frustrated by the mother's answers, so she turned to the boy and asked if he
thought he'd died. "Sure," the boy replied cheerfully.
"That's what everyone says." The frame froze on the
smiling image of the boy, and the reporter's voice
intoned, "However, that's not what everyone says."

The picture cut away to a somber-looking man.
The caption at the bottom of the screen identified

him as Dr. Voinovich, and he began to explain what happened to Luke Quinn on the day of "the miracle." The nurse put down the chart and and listened. To her surprise, the doctor said the boy had never actually been dead on the day in question.

"Not dead?" said the woman reporter. "But then how can you explain the fact that he showed no vital signs for nearly two hours?"

"A phenomena called the Mammalian Diving Reflex," said the doctor. "It's rare, but there have been other similar cases. When the conditions are exactly right, as they were in this instance, it is possible for the human body to go into a state of suspended animation—much the same idea as a computer going to sleep. No outward signs of life, but the body is still functioning on a barely detectable level."

"Fascinating," said the reporter.

"Once the body temperature is restored to near normal, the brain reactivates the vital functions. We've studied the medical data on the boy, and this is clearly what occurred in this case."

The nurse shook her head, trying to grasp this information.

The reporter on television asked, "So it was not a miracle?"

"No," said the doctor emphatically, "it was

most certainly not a miracle."

Dr. Cheung appeared in the doorway. He glanced at the television and asked, "What's this?"

"*Inside Look*," answered the nurse. "They've got a show on about Ms. Carey's son—I thought she'd like to watch it."

Dr. Cheung smiled patiently. "That's considerate of you, Karen, but it's highly unlikely she can hear any of this."

"You never know," replied the nurse. "Might do her good."

Dr. Cheung shrugged. "It's possible, I suppose."

Suddenly, there was the sound of shouting from the television: "Get out!" Startled, Cheung and the nurse looked at the screen and saw the image of Josh Carey, his face distorted in anger. "Get out," he said quietly, still mad. Dr. Cheung and the nurse looked at each other questioningly. "What the—?" muttered the doctor under his breath. He moved to the television and turned up the sound. In the exchange that followed, Josh alternately fumbled for words and snapped at the reporter.

Cheung shook his head. "This makes no sense," he said.

The reporter asked Josh if he had a Christ

complex and he replied, "Sure, I'm the Risen Lord." This clip was played in an overlapping fashion two more times, finally freezing on a blurred image of Josh, his eyes wild.

"This is crazy," said Dr. Cheung. "They're cruficing him."

Dr. Cheung and the nurse watched in horror as the woman reporter finished with an editorial about the danger of false messiahs. Cheung shook his head in silent anger and was about to turn off the television, when suddenly the heart monitor sounded an alarm. Cheung moved quickly to the bed and hit the intercom on the nightstand.

"Get the defibrillator in here, fast!" he shouted into the speaker. "We have a code blue!"

Cheung waved the nurse toward the bed. "Help me," he said. The nurse tore back the bed sheets, and the doctor began to pump rhythmically on the old woman's chest. After his first exertions, he paused for a moment to catch his breath.

"There's no pulse," whispered the nurse nervously.

Cheung nodded grimly and again applied pressure to the old woman's chest in steady, measured beats as the monitor alarm continued to pierce the air.

29

Sarah switched off the television and tossed the remote on the coffee table. Luke looked at his mother, trying to gauge her mood.

"So," he began tentatively, "I didn't die after all?"

Sarah stared into space, her mind elsewhere.

"Mom," said Luke. "My hair's on fire."

"That's nice, honey," said Sarah.

Luke clapped his hands loudly in front of his mother's face, startling her. "I asked you something important. Did you hear me?"

"What?"

"Did I die, or not?" demanded Luke.

"Apparently not, sweetheart," said Sarah, running her hand through her son's hair. "Thank goodness, miracle or no miracle, you didn't."

Luke thought about this for a second. "So

I guess we won't be famous anymore," he said finally.

"Oh, I hope not, Luke," said Sarah. "I've had enough of being famous for one lifetime."

"Me, too," said Luke. "I'm tired of being the Amazing Undead Kid."

Sarah laughed quietly and put her arm around her son.

"Why did they make Josh look crazy?" asked Luke. "He's not like that at all."

Sarah shook her head sadly. "I don't know. Because they're awful people. Because it makes a better story, even if it isn't true."

Luke nodded, taking this in. "Should we call him?"

Sarah hesitated before saying, "I'm not sure that would be a good idea, honey."

"Why not?"

"Oh," said Sarah, "he's probably as upset about the show as we are."

"All the more reason to call him," said Luke.

As if on cue, the phone began to ring. Luke looked at his mother. "Maybe that's him now," he said. He ran to the phone, answered it, and listened as the person on the other end spoke. A look of disappointment crossed his face, and he held the phone out to Sarah. "It's for you."

Puzzled, Sarah took the phone from him. "Yes?" she said into the phone.

"Ms. Quinn, this is Andrew Aikens from the *Times*," said the voice on the line. "Would you care to make a comment on this evening's broadcast on *Inside Story*?"

Sarah's face flushed with anger. "No," she said. "No, I wouldn't. And please don't call this number again." She slammed the phone into its cradle. Almost immediately, it began to ring again. Luke gestured that she should answer it, but she shook her head. The answering machine in the kitchen picked up, and they could hear it was a call from another reporter. Shaking her head furiously, Sarah unplugged the living room phone, and walked quickly to the kitchen to unplug the wall phone. As soon as she had done this, she and Luke could hear the upstairs extensions ringing with a new call. She made a move toward the stairs, but Luke held up his hand to stop her.

"I'll do it," he said, and ran up the stairs. Sarah walked back into the living room and slumped onto the couch, as the sound of ringing phones continued to echo through the house.

30

The headline of the newspaper on the nightstand read "From Messiah to Pariah." Josh picked up the paper and read the first few paragraphs. The story described the events of the previous night's broadcast on *Inside Look*, and how he'd been exposed as a fake miracle worker. Josh skimmed the rest of the story and felt oddly distant from the whole thing. It was almost as if he were reading about someone he barely knew. In the last paragraph was the cryptic sentence, "Calls from this reporter to Mr. Carey were not returned." Josh was unaware that anyone had tried to reach him because he'd been at the hospital all night with his mother. It seemed that even his silence was being used against him. *What could I have said, anyhow?* he wondered. He had clearly been tried and found guilty. In the article there was a picture of him, taken from the television interview, that made him look half-mad. *Well, perhaps I am nuts,* he thought. *Perhaps this is all just some sort of hallucination.*

Dr. Cheung walked into the room and saw Josh reading the paper. "Josh," he said, "why are you reading that garbage? Don't you already have enough to worry about?"

Josh nodded and put the paper back on the sidetable. He looked at his mother, who was lying in the bed breathing shallowly, and then up at Cheung. "Have you gotten the test results back yet?" he asked.

Cheung shook his head. "Not yet. We'll have them in a couple of hours."

"Okay."

"But I have to tell you, as a doctor and your friend," said Cheung, "you must prepare yourself for the worst. I believe your mother has lapsed into an irreversible coma and that there is almost no chance she will recover."

The words hit Josh like a hammer blow, and he slumped into his chair. For a moment, neither man said anything. The only sound was the cheerful version of "We Wish You a Merry Christmas" playing on the hospital's PA system in the hallway.

Cheung stepped forward and put his hand on

Josh's shoulder. "I'm sorry, Josh," he said softly.

Josh nodded. Cheung lingered for a moment, but then turned and left the room. Josh looked at his mother and then leaned forward in his chair, taking her left hand in his. He stared at the blue veins streaking her hands and the long, delicate fingers curved by arthritis. *I have done everything I can, Mom,* he thought sadly. *I wish to God I could bring you back, but I don't know how to do that.*

He gently released her hand and sank back into his chair, staring out the window at the school yard Santa. It had been battered by the winds and had lost some air. He watched as the Santa danced in the breeze, its head flopping like a chicken with a broken neck. *So now I'm a national joke,* he mused. *The miracle worker who can't work miracles.* He turned back to his mother and was startled to see that her eyes were open. When he recovered from his shock, he looked deeply into his mother's eyes to see if there was life in them. She began to shake her head on the pillow.

"What were you thinking, giving that interview?" she said in a raspy voice.

Josh froze in his chair. "Mom," he said warily, "are you speaking to me, or am I imagining this?"

His mother smiled at him patiently and said,

"What do you think I am? A ghost?"

"But—" Josh stammered, "this isn't possible— you are—were—in a coma."

"Not now," replied his mother. "Another one of your miracles."

"Really?" said Josh in amazement.

"Of course not," said his mother, winking. "Didn't you watch the show? It's been pretty well established you're no miracle worker."

"That's true," said Josh with a smile.

"I'm starving," said Josh's mother. "Who's in charge of the food around here? I'd kill for a steak."

31

$\mathcal{D}$elia stood in Jack Reardon's doorway and waved a sheaf of papers. "Did you see these numbers?" she asked with unconcealed delight.

Reardon looked up and smiled pleasantly. "Yes, they're lovely," he said.

"Lovely?" said Delia in mock anger. "Jack, we haven't seen ratings like this since the sextuplets show. Not even close."

"Extraordinary," said Reardon, nodding.

"I have to say you called it on this one," said Delia. "I hate to admit you were right, but you were. I never should have doubted you."

"No," replied Reardon thoughtfully.

"I think we should do a follow-up show, don't you?" said Delia. "We've been inundated with calls and letters. Perhaps we could do a whole investigative series about religious charlatans and phony messiahs. It'd be—I don't know—a public service."

"Yes, that is an idea," said Reardon vaguely.

Delia was struck by the odd tone in Reardon's voice, and she gave him a quizzical look. "What's with you, Jack? Aren't you feeling well?"

"Au contraire, my little minx," said Reardon, shuffling some papers on his desk. "I feel in the proverbial pink—why do you ask?"

"Because you're not reacting as I thought you would," said Delia. She moved closer to his desk. "Normally, you'd be all over this thing like a cheap suit—what gives?"

"Ah, well, yes," said Reardon. "In theory, I am all over this like a cheap suit, but in actual practice I am not."

Delia stared at him, trying to make sense of his words. "Are we talking in Esperanto today?"

"No," said Reardon. "English is just fine."

"So are you game?" asked Delia, pressing her point. "Let's trigger a follow-up show right away."

Reardon shifted uncomfortably in his chair. "No, I don't think we'll do that."

"That's insane," said Delia. "If we don't do a follow-up on this Josh Carey thing, we're morons. Can you explain to me why we wouldn't?"

Reardon stared at her evenly for a moment

and then straightened in his chair. "I was hoping to put this off until after the holidays," he said, "but there's no time like the present, I suppose. Sit down, Delia."

Delia felt the muscles in her neck tense. Warily, with her eyes fixed on Reardon, she moved to the couch and sat down. "Jack, what's going on?"

"Well, we have a little problem," said Reardon in a neutral voice.

"What kind of problem?" demanded Delia. "Doesn't this network like high ratings anymore?"

"No, it's not the ratings. The ratings are fabulous," said Reardon. "Everyone loves the ratings; that's beyond dispute." He paused to take a swig from the Evian bottle on his desk. "Problem is," he continued, "not everyone loved the show."

"That's crazy," said Delia dismissively. "The calls and letters we're getting are overwhelmingly in favor of the show. So what if a few nutcases didn't like it—who cares?"

"Ah, yes, well, I wish it were that easy," said Reardon, putting the cap back on the water bottle. "Unfortunately, one very important viewer didn't care at all for the show—the Chairman's wife."

Delia's heart began to race. "The Chairman's wife?" she said hoarsely, her throat suddenly very dry.

"Yes," said Reardon, shaking his head sadly. "Seems she really hated it—and not just a little. A lot."

Delia felt light-headed and steadied herself against the arm of the couch. "Do we know why?" she asked in a whisper.

"I didn't at first," said Reardon. "But I do now after the Chairman spent the better part of an hour screaming at me. I must say, he has a very colorful vocabulary."

Delia leaned forward with urgency. "The Chairman's wife, Jack," she pressed. "Why did she hate the show so much?"

"Where does one begin?" wondered Reardon aloud. "I mean, there were just so many things. But the short version, I suppose, is that Mrs. Chairman recently and unexpectedly found God."

"Found God?" said Delia weakly.

"Yes," said Reardon wearily. "Mrs. Chairman has been—what do you call it?"

"Born again?"

"Yes, that's it," said Reardon. "She's apparently become quite fanatical about this whole Jesus thing. And she didn't appreciate your story. She felt you were making fun of religion."

"I wasn't, Jack," Delia protested. "You know

that. I hope you defended me."

"Oh, to the bitter end," said Reardon, nodding vigorously. "I defended you with all my might. I told the Chairman you have great respect for religion, and Jesus, and all that. But I'm afraid this cut very little mustard with him. It would seem he's gotten an earful from Mrs. Chairman."

An ominous thought clouded Delia's mind. "Did he fire you?"

Reardon laughed. "Oh, no, my pet," he said, waving away her concerns. "Nothing so dramatic as all that. My job, at least for the moment, is secure."

Delia breathed a sigh of relief. "That's good. You had me worried for a minute there."

"However," said Reardon, "we may have to make a few structural changes within the show."

"Structural changes?"

"Yes," said Reardon. "Nothing to be alarmed about. What would you think about covering the celebrity beat for a while?

Delia's blood froze. "Celebrity beat?" she said in disbelief. "You have to be joking."

"I'm perfectly serious," said Reardon, shuffling some papers on his desk. "It might be a nice change of pace for you."

"Jack, don't do this to me," Delia pleaded. "I'm a journalist, not a gossip monger."

"Well, I'm afraid this is our only option," said Reardon. "The Chairman was most adamant you be taken off serious news. I fought for you—valiantly, like a tiger, you would have been proud. But in the end, it was a losing battle, I'm sorry to report."

Delia stared at Jack in shock, trying to make sense of what he had just told her. "And if I don't agree to cover the celebrity beat," Delia said tentatively, "what happens then?"

Reardon squirmed in his chair. "Let's just say that's an option I'd prefer not to explore—it being Christmastime and all."

"Are you saying you'd fire me?" said Delia, anger rising in her voice.

"That's such an ugly word," said Reardon.

"I'm not going to cover the celebrity beat, Jack," said Delia. "Why are you doing this to me?"

"What I'm doing to you, my little smiling viper, is saving your job," said Reardon, banging his hand on the desk. "What I'm doing is saving you from being kicked to the curb at Christmas."

"Jack—" said Delia helplessly.

"Now, let's get down to brass tacks," said Reardon, rubbing his hands together. "Why don't you take a few extra days off at Christmas? Rest up, refill the well, and all that."

"Jack—" pleaded Delia.

Reardon ignored her and continued. "We want you rested for New Year's. There's a new casino opening in Vegas, and I'd like you to be there to cover it, all right?"

Delia tried to speak, but no words came out.

"Positively everyone is going to be there," said Reardon with relish. "A wonderful way to kick off this new phase of your career. I have it on good authority the Hilton sisters may even put in an appearance. What fun, eh?"

32

Josh stood in the middle of the street, looking at the snow drifting down. In the distance, he could hear faint voices singing "Good King Wenceslas." Carolers? A car radio? Looking skyward, he let the soft, wet snowflakes land upon his face. He reached into his coat pockets for his gloves and realized he had forgotten them at home. He smiled at the blanket of white stretched out before him and impulsively reached down to scoop up a big handful of newly fallen snow. It felt pleasantly brisk on his bare hands. He packed it tight into a perfect snowball and admired his handiwork. He looked around for a suitable target and then hurled the snowball at the stop sign at the end of the street. The snowball arced silently out of the glow of the streetlight, disappeared for a few seconds, and then smashed to the ground twenty feet short of the stop sign.

Josh exhaled happily, watching the steam from his breath float upward into the night air. For the first time in weeks, he felt like himself again. He caught a brief glimpse of the moon and a few stars peeking through the fast-moving clouds. Gathering up another handful of snow, he hurled a second snowball in the direction of the stop sign. This one landed closer to the sign, about ten feet away. As he gathered up more snow, he heard a voice: "Hey—what're you doing?"

Josh looked over and saw Luke standing on the upstairs balcony of the Quinn home. The boy was leaning on the rail, his shoulders hunched up against the cold. Josh shrugged and said, "I'm getting ready for baseball season."

Luke laughed. "Are you going to stay out there, or are you going to come in?"

"I haven't made up my mind yet," said Josh.

"I think you should come in," said Luke.

"I'm not sure your mother wants to see me."

"Only one way to find out." The boy waved and then went back into the house.

Josh watched him go and then packed the snow in his hands. When the snowball was perfectly round, he threw it into the night air. It flew in a line drive and hit the stop sign with a satisfying clang. The sign vibrated for a couple of seconds and then was still. Josh stood in the middle of the street, wondering what he should do. Taking a deep breath, he turned and walked slowly up the driveway to the Quinn home.

When he got to the front stoop, he reached for the knocker, but the door swung open, and he found himself facing Sarah.

Before he could stop himself, he said, "If you don't want to talk to me, I understand."

Sarah frowned and tilted her head. "What are you talking about?" she asked.

"The whole interview mess. It's my fault," said Josh. "If you don't want to talk to me, or see me ever again, I understand."

"Well," said Sarah, "you *are* the most unpopular man in America at the moment. I'll have to think about it."

"I'm serious," said Josh, "I feel terrible about everything. I should have listened to you. You were right, and I was wrong. What can I do to make it up to you?"

Sarah took Josh's face in her hands and kissed him. After a moment, she drew back and said, "You could buy me dinner."

For a moment, Josh was too surprised to speak.

As the shock of the kiss wore off, he said finally, "Are you joking?"

"I never joke about dinner," said Sarah. "Let me get my coat."

Josh stood in the doorway, watching her. She took a few steps before turning back to him and extending her hand. Smiling, he took her hand and followed her into the house.

33

$\mathcal{L}$uther atc his dinner from a folding tray, muttering curses at the television set. Toby sat at his feet, watching him eat. The newscaster on television was in the middle of an editorial about Josh Carey and false prophets. Luther put a bite of steak in his mouth and shook his head in disgust.

"First, they say he's a miracle worker. Then, they say he's a liar," said Luther. "I wish these geniuses would make up their minds."

Toby heard the emotion in his owner's voice, and he barked excitely. He assumed Luther's words had something to do with food, since all he thought about was food.

Luther saw the dog's barking as a sign of agreement. "But you and I know what happened, don't we, boy?" he said. "You're my miracle dog."

Toby barked again and opened his mouth to

show he was ready for a treat. Just then the phone in the kitchen rang. Luther threw his napkin on the tray and went to answer it. Toby watched him go and moved closer to the tray. The steak was inches away, at eye level, temptingly close. Toby looked in the kitchen and saw Luther had his back turned. Making up his mind, Toby reached forward and grasped the steak between his teeth. With a quick flick of his head, he yanked the steak off the plate. This motion shook the tray, which wobbled for a second, and then crashed onto the floor.

Luther turned at the noise and saw Toby standing in the middle of the living room with the steak between his teeth. "What's going on?" said Luther, flaring. "I gotta call you back," he shouted to the caller and hung up the phone. He moved toward Toby, and the dog watched him uncertainly, trying to gauge his master's mood. Luther stepped into the living room, and the two of them stood motionless, sizing each other up. Suddenly, Luther lunged for Toby, but the dog danced quickly out of the way. Luther made another grab for the dog, but in doing so he caught his foot on the carpet and crashed to the floor. The noise of Luther falling startled Toby so much he almost dropped the steak. He turned quickly and bolted through the plastic dog door.

Luther made a last futile grab for him, but Toby and the steak were gone.

"So much for man's best friend," Luther grumbled to himself. "Well, I guess it's true what they say: the Lord helps those who help themselves."

34

The snow was falling heavily by the time Josh steered his truck onto the main road. As he turned, the back tires fishtailed a few feet before catching the road. Sarah looked at Josh's profile in the dim dashboard light. She couldn't put her finger on it, but something about him seemed different.

"So what do you do now?" she asked.

"I don't know," answered Josh. "The last few days have shot my faith-healing business to pieces."

Sarah smiled. "Seriously—where do you go from here?"

"Go back to the way things were before, if people will let me," Josh said. "I never asked for any of this, you know."

"I know," said Sarah softly.

"The only good that came out of this circus was

that I met you," said Josh. "That makes it worth-
while."

Sarah's eyes welled with tears. "Yes," she said,
"it does."

Josh glanced at her and smiled happily. Suddenly, something darted from the side of the road
into the headlights. There was a dull thump, and
the truck shuddered.

"What was that?" cried Sarah in alarm. "Did
you run over a tree branch?"

"No, I hit something," said Josh. He steered
the truck over to the side and did a wide, looping
U-turn back in the direction they had come. In
the headlights, Josh and Sarah could see an animal's body lying by the side of the road. Sarah
looked nervously at Josh as he pulled onto the
shoulder and killed the engine. Cautiously, they
climbed out of the cab and walked toward the
motionless animal. The falling snow was so thick
it was hard at first to tell what sort of creature
it was. Its back was arched in an unnatural position, clearly broken. When they drew closer to
the animal, Josh realized it was a dog—Luther
Froebler's dog, Toby.

"Oh, no," moaned Josh. "I know this dog. I
mean, I know the owner."

"Josh, I'm so sorry," said Sarah. "Is he dead?"

Josh looked carefully at the dog. Its eyes were blank, and there was a small trickle of blood at the corner of its mouth. "Yes," said Josh finally. "I'm afraid he's very dead."

"This is terrible," said Sarah. "What do we do?"

Josh shrugged helplessly. "Nothing to do but take the body home and face the music. I feel horrible. Luther just loved this dog."

Sarah put a sympathetic hand on Josh's arm. With a sigh, he kneeled down and gathered the dead dog in his arms. The dog was heavy, perhaps eighty pounds, and it was an effort to lift him. As Josh started to rise, the dog's body lurched in his arms in what seemed to be some sort of after-death spasm. However, when Josh stood up, the dog's movements grew more furious, and the body slipped from his hands. Seeing this, Sarah cried out. Josh tried to catch the body, but it fell to the ground. The dog landed on its feet and stood staring at them.

Spooked, Sarah took a couple of steps backward. "Josh," she said cautiously, "what's going on?"

"I don't know," replied Josh, who looked at his hands in bewilderment and then back at Sarah.

"But I'm getting the idea that somebody's trying to tell me something."

The dog looked at the two of them and then gave a sharp bark, as if reprimanding them. He then turned and ran off into the night. Speechless, Josh and Sarah watched the dog disappear into the grove of trees that lined the road.

After a long moment, Sarah turned to Josh. "I thought you said the dog was dead."

"It was," Josh insisted.

Sarah shook her head in disbelief. "But if it was dead—" she began, "then you must have—then you *do* have . . ." She let the thought dangle unspoken in the air.

Josh nodded, his mind reeling with the implications of what had just happened. He and Sarah stared at each other as the snow drifted down around them. After a few seconds, he raised his hands and said, "Let's not tell anyone about this, okay?"

Sarah nodded. "Sure," she said, "but—"

"Anyone," said Josh firmly.

Sarah smiled. Josh reached out and took her arm, and they walked back to the truck through the falling snow.

About the Author

Photo by Claire Parkin

*J*udd Parkin was born in Chicago, Illinois. He is an award-winning producer and screenwriter whose many credits include the films *Jesus, Nicholas' Gift*, and *Comfort and Joy*. He lives in Los Angeles with his wife, Marilyn, and is the proud father of Claire, Hilary, and Sam.

Visit Judd's website at jlparkin.com for more information.